Economic Influences on the Development of Accounting in Firms

A view of accounting as a practical activity – a service function whose value depends on its adaptation to the environment in which it serves – is a good place to start this book, originally published in 1996. While arts such as music and drama can be said to serve human needs, their development presumably cannot be explained primarily by reference to the economic features of their environments. By contrast, an economic service function such as accounting develops in response to economic features of its environment. The objective of this book is to stimulate interest in explaining the development of specific features of accounting as we know it in the firms that are so important to the economies of Western industrialized countries by reference to the economic features of those firms. The emphasis in this work is on the influence of economic features of the firm in the development of accounting.

Economic Influences on the Development of Accounting in Firms

George J. Staubus

Routledge
Taylor & Francis Group

First published in 1996
by Garland Publishing Inc.

This edition first published in 2021 by Routledge
2 Park Square, Milton Park, Abingdon, Oxon OX14 4RN

and by Routledge
52 Vanderbilt Avenue, New York, NY 10017

Routledge is an imprint of the Taylor & Francis Group, an informa business

Publisher's Note
The publisher has gone to great lengths to ensure the quality of this reprint but
points out that some imperfections in the original copies may be apparent.

Disclaimer
The publisher has made every effort to trace copyright holders and welcomes
correspondence from those they have been unable to contact.

A Library of Congress record exists under ISBN: 081532247X

ISBN: 978-0-367-72125-1 (hbk)
ISBN: 978-1-003-15354-2 (ebk)

Economic Influences on the Development of Accounting in Firms

George J. Staubus

Garland Publishing, Inc.
New York and London 1996

Library of Congress Cataloging-in-Publication Data

Staubus, George J.
   Economic influences on the development of accounting in firms /
George J. Staubus.
      p. cm. — (New works in accounting history)
   Includes bibliographical references and index.
   ISBN 0-8153-2247-X
   1. Corporations—Accounting—History. 2. Financial statements—
History. I. Title. II. Series
HF5686.C7S735   1996   95–46813
657—dc20   CIP

All volumes printed on acid-free, 250-year-life paper.
Manufactured in the United States of America.

Design by Marisel Tavarez

To

Janette
Lindsay
Martin
Paul

CONTENTS

ECONOMIC INFLUENCES ON THE DEVELOPMENT OF ACCOUNTING IN FIRMS

INTRODUCTION

Double entry developed in Italy in response to the needs of nascent capitalism.

(de Roover, 1956, p. 174)

A view of accounting as a practical activity -- a service function whose value depends on its adaptation to the environment in which it serves -- is a good place to start this book. While arts such as music and drama can be said to serve human needs, their development presumably cannot be explained primarily by reference to the economic features of their environments. In a different field, the laws that govern chemical reactions take into consideration physical features of the environment, but not economic features. By contrast, an economic service function such as accounting develops in response to economic features of its environment.

Firm accounting has developed to measure and report the effects of economic events on the firm. A premise of this investigation is that one's ability to understand and explain the development of a particular firm's accounting policies and practices is enhanced by an understanding of the economics of firms in general and of that firm in particular. Both firms and accounting have existed for a long time, and they developed together over many centuries. By present-day standards, these developments occurred very slowly prior to the mercantile revolution and advancement of knowledge during the Renaissance, roughly the fourteenth through sixteenth centuries in Europe. After a lull, the pace picked up again during the series of economic revolutions of the late eighteenth, nineteenth and early twentieth centuries. After the great depression of the 1930s, the development of firms accelerated again. Some observers, e.g. Johnson and Kaplan (1987, pp. 195-204), question whether accounting has kept pace.

The objective of this book is to stimulate interest in explaining the development of specific features of accounting as we know it in the firms that are so important to the economies of Western industrialized countries by reference to the economic features of those firms. Because the development of the prototypical large firm and its accounting system took place in the century ending with the great depression, many of the developments of interest here occurred during that era, but developments before and after that period are also important. General influences on the development of accounting over many centuries, such as literacy, numeracy, money, credit, capital, uncertainty, incomplete markets and imperfect markets are not included here; they are viewed as exogenous influences. The emphasis here is on endogenous influences.

The research techniques employed here are "soft." Library resources and personal experience are drawn on to identify features of firms and their activities that are important to the development of accounting and to make connections between those features and specific accounting principles. The degree of clarity with which those connections are perceived cannot be measured; a reader with a different background may encounter more or less haze than is indicated here. Each of the specific propositions stated at the ends of the subsections is intended to be descriptive of a connection between a feature of the firm and an accounting development. Value judgments are avoided. The propositions do, however, vary in the degree of conviction with which they are believed by the author. Many are likely to be viewed by the reader as so obvious as to be mundane; others are so speculative that they will be viewed as hypotheses requiring careful research before they are accepted -- or rejected. Readers' interpretations along this scale are bound to vary. Unfortunately, the reader who demands incontrovertible support for positions taken will be disappointed.

The emphasis in this work is on the influence of economic features of the firm in the development of accounting. At various points along the way, a question may arise regarding influence in the opposite direction. For example, large firm size is seen to have influenced the development of accounting in several ways. However, accounting surely has raised the upper limit of viable firm size. Several such reverse influences are identified herein, but no special effort is made to show the contributions that accounting has made to the development of firms.

The main part of the book is organized around features of firms. First a definition of the firm is offered and some implications of that definition for accounting are suggested. The most basic features of firms not covered in the definition are referred to as tier I influences: bounded rationality of managers, the prevalence of self-interested (opportunistic) behavior, firm uniqueness, externalities and the dilution of cost/benefit consequences, information losses in transmission, and indivisibilities and economies of scale in acquisition of resources. Tier II influences, which differ only in that they are perceived as resting somewhat on tier I influences, include cost of information, asset specificity and nonredeployability, performance evaluation and incentive plans, and conflicts of interests. Tier III influences, which rest on tier I and tier II considerations, are most closely related to developments in firm accounting. They are size, vertical integration, diversification, and organization form. Each of these fourteen features of firms is examined and its probable influences on accounting are identified. Certain of these features are developed more fully than others because they are perceived to be either more influential or more neglected in the literature of accounting. A one-page diagrammatic listing of the features of firms that have influenced accounting appears at the end of the book.

CHAPTER 1
THE NATURE OF THE FIRM

The most pervasive premise for this investigation is that the major features of firm accounting as we know it today evolved in the second millennium, CE, in firms.[1] Some observers would emphasize the development of double-entry bookkeeping in the fourteenth and fifteenth centuries; others would focus on the rise of the joint stock company; still others would say that accounting as we know it jelled in the century ending in 1939. All of these views are consistent with the premise that firms and accounting evolved together, even if they were not conceived as twins. If that notion is true, the nature of the firm must be intimately related to the nature of accounting.

What is "the nature of the firm"? Since publication of Ronald Coase's seminal paper with that title (1937) -- in fact, even in that paper -- various features of the firm have been emphasized in the literature of economics and accounting. Different authors have focused on different features. Some have then accepted one feature as so central as to justify building a theory of the firm or a theory of accounting around it.

This chapter commences with a light survey of literature dealing with concepts of the firm, including observations on the suitability of each concept as an aid in understanding the development of firm accounting. Next, a definition of the firm consistent with the interpretation that I speculate prevailed during accounting's formative centuries is proposed. Finally, some implications of that view of the firm for accounting are suggested.

A REVIEW OF VIEWS

The Contracting Theme

"The essence of the classical firm is identified here as a contractual structure with" various specified parties, relationships, and rights, especially a "central agent ... called the firm's owner and the employer." (Alchian and Demsetz, 1972, p. 794) They emphasized the central agent's contracts with owners of the other inputs and the residual rights of that agent. Outputs and customers were ignored as were a motive for forming a firm and conditions for its continued existence. Jensen and Meckling criticized Alchian and Demsetz for overemphasis on the role of joint inputs and for neglect of customers, then presented their well-known definition of the firm that stressed a "legal fiction which serves as a nexus for contracting relationships." (1976, p. 311) They, too, ignored motivation and conditions for continuation.

A few accountants, notably Butterworth, Gibbins and King (1982, pp. 11-29), Watts and Zimmerman (1986, pp. 193-8), and Ball (1989, p. 2) have accepted the contracting role of the firm as critical, but most have not. Only Ball has given serious consideration to contracting in defining the firm. "The economic role of the firm is modelled as a specialist contracting intermediary, intermediating between consumers and suppliers of factors of production, exploiting scale economies in repetitive contracting by centralizing contracting in one institution." (p. 2) Ball and Smith (1992, p. 3) have taken the strongest position on the relationship between contracting and accounting:

> In principle, the economics of costly contracting, modified to allow for economic regulation, can be used to explain the existence of accounting, the form taken by the profession, the existence of GAAP, the process that determines GAAP, the content of GAAP, the

selection of GAAP by corporations, and the most detailed institutional facts in accounting.

Neither the emphasis on contracting in defining the firm nor its appeal to accountants as the key link between firms and accounting is easy to explain. First, consider the extent of contracting in firm activities. Firms contract with factor suppliers and other providers of inputs and with customers. Those *transactions* are important events in the lives of firms. But so are all of the internal activities -- *intra-actions* (Staubus, 1961, p. 60) -- not involving contracts that go on inside integrated firms as resources are combined to make various products. Indeed, the view of the integrated firm as a substitute for market relationships (Coase, 1937, pp. 390-3) (1) puts more emphasis on the role of accounting information in the noncontractual, internal operations than in actual contracting, and (2) suggests that, for a given volume of economic activity, fewer contracts are made if that activity is integrated into one firm than if it is spread over many firms that contract with each other. Contracting and market prices characterize entries of resources and exits of products. Management decisions using cost accounting data and information from many other sources guide the combining of resources into products within the firm.

Another consideration in evaluating the emphasis on contracting in explaining the role of accounting in firms is the frequency with which a firm's contracts depend on conventional accounting (in monetary units). One type of customer contract does so depend: "cost-plus" contracts. Most, however, do not - - except to the extent that costs may indirectly influence market prices. A few contracts with suppliers of factors, commodities, and services also depend on accounting numbers: certain loan agreements include accounting-based covenants, a few employment contracts provide for earnings-based bonuses, and the occasional lease depends on sales or income. Most, however, do not, and certainly did not during firm accounting's formative decades. A manager's use of accounting information in forming judgments on matters such as product prices and resource prices presumably are not thought of as uses of accounting numbers in contracting; they exemplify the conventional uses of accounting information in making decisions. In most firms, the aggregate value of accounting information in these noncontracting uses surely is greater than that in contracting uses. Indeed, the market prices specified in contracts are more important as inputs to accounting than accounting numbers are as components of contracts. Putting it all together, contracting is an important activity of firms, and contracts are important as sources and uses of accounting information, but there must have been other features of firms that had more influence on the development of accounting. One such feature was conflicts of interests -- including those between contracting parties -- which receive a great deal of attention in a subsequent chapter.

A Coalition, A System of Relationships

This theme began with Coase: "A firm ... consists of the system of relationships which comes into existence when the direction of resources is dependent on an entrepreneur." (1937, p. 393) This statement was made in the context of a discussion of market organization vs. firm organization of a set of activities. Related economic activities may be connected by market transactions or by intrafirm relationships. When a set of activities is integrated in a firm, the "visible hand" of management (Chandler, 1977) replaces the invisible hand of markets. (Smith, 1776) Coase was interested in explaining why markets prevailed in some cases, firms in others. But note that two additional features are included: resources, and direction by an entrepreneur. One could focus on either of those features and claim a Coasian view. Still another Coasian view is set forth in a subsequent section.

Alchian and Woodward picked up the relationships feature and added two others. "The classic, paradigmatic private property firm is a coalition among owners of separately owned resources whose value as a team exceeds the sum of the market values each could get separately." (1988, p. 70) Mention of owners is a step towards recognition of constituents, although customers are still ignored. The reference to excess value is a step towards recognition of a motive for organizing a firm.

The Firm as a Governance Structure

Williamson distinguishes three principal governance structures to which transactions might be assigned: firm, market and hybrid modes. (1988, p. 12) This view is in sharp contrast to the contracting view. "... [T]ransaction cost economics regards the firm as a governance structure and agency theory considers it a nexus of contracts." (1987, p. 5) Again, "... the business firm is not regarded as a neoclassical production function but is described instead as a governance structure -- the internal structure, incentives, and controls of which matter." (1989, p. 14) The emphasis here is on internal relationships and activities rather than contracting in markets. The governance structure that operates to organize activities within a firm rather than across markets is characterized by phenomena such as budgeting, personnel policies, performance reporting, promotion criteria, transfer pricing, capital budgeting procedures, organization charts, and exchanges of favors. By this view, firms substitute internal governance procedures for market contracting. In this context, it seems odd to suggest (cf. Ball, 1989) that switching from market transactions (contracts) to noncontractual, in-firm intra-actions puts more emphasis on contracting. Of course, a firm still must have contacts, and contracts, with suppliers of resources and with customers. But as between the organization of a hundred activities necessary to make a consumer good (a), in one firm or (b) in a hundred economic units, the former requires fewer contracts because intermediates are transferred between activities in the firm without a contract. Needless to say, the real firms with which accountants are concerned these days tend to involve from dozens to thousands of integrated activities.

Is the role of the firm as a governance structure the feature that is most important to accounting? To an economist concerned with the organization of the economy, whether activities are combined in an integrated firm or separated in small units is of considerable import. But the accountant focuses on one economic unit. Its relationships with the economic system are called transactions, each one with specific goods, price, quantity, and counterparty characteristics. What the integration feature of firms adds to accounting's role is the duty of providing information to guide and report on internal relationships.

Supersession of Price Mechanism

"It can, I think, be assumed that the distinguishing mark of the firm is the supersession of the price mechanism." (Coase, 1937, p. 389) Coase was concerned about the " ... gap in economic theory between the assumption (made for some purposes) that resources are allocated by means of the price mechanism and the assumption (made for other purposes) that this allocation is dependent on the entrepreneur-co-ordinator." He went on to inquire as to " ... why a firm emerges at all in a specialized exchange economy." (p. 390) His answer -- "There is a cost of using the price mechanism" -- laid a cornerstone for transaction cost economics. "We may sum up ... by saying that the operation of a market costs something and by forming an organization and allowing some authority (an "entrepreneur") to direct the resources, certain marketing costs are saved." (p. 392) How far can such integrating steps go? " ... [A] firm will tend to expand until the costs of organizing an extra transaction within the firm become equal to the costs of carrying out the same transaction by means of an exchange on the open market or the costs of organizing in another firm." (p. 395)

The idea of comparing "the cost and value of 'quasi-price' information provided by cost accounting in vertically integrated firms (with) the cost and value of prices provided by markets to nonintegrated firms" (Staubus, 1988, p. 247) is intriguing. Coase expresses it well: "While outside the firm prices, and therefore costs, are explicit ... and are determined by the operations of the market, within the firm there are explicit costs for exactly the same reason, but they are provided by the accounting system. This internal system takes the place of the pricing system of the market." (1990, p. 9) The view that the firm supersedes the price mechanism in directing the uses of resources casts accounting in a leading role: providing the numbers to guide intra-firm resource allocations.

The Management-Centric Firm

All of the other constituents of a firm may see the management as representing the firm. In a mature firm with no concentrated ownership interest, the top management group deals with all other "stakeholders" in obtaining their cooperation as suppliers of resources and customers, despite conflicts of interests. Like the chairman of a committee, management must offer enough to each participant to obtain its continued participation, preferably with a positive attitude. Management may be described as the glue that holds the coalition together. Or, using the atom analogy, management is the nucleus around which all of the constituent electrons revolve. It is supported by a management information system. Accounting has developed to serve management as part of that information system.

A Collection of Assets

"We define the firm as being composed of the assets (e.g., machines, inventories) that it owns." (Grossman and Hart, 1986, p. 692) This simple definition focuses on a subject that is dear to the hearts of accountants, but they might also find it lacking. Buchanan had stated a much broader view long before. "... (T)he most common and obvious implication of the term 'business enterprise' is that of an aggregation of assets devoted to the earning of profits in which certain individuals possess rather well-defined rights." (1940, p. 15)

The rights of other parties suggest liabilities as well as various constituents. The profit motive adds another important dimension. Assets, obligations, constituents, and a profit motive might be viewed as traditional features of a firm, but assets alone are not enough.

The Asset Specificity Rationale

"The whole rationale for the employer-employee status, and even for the existence of firms, rests on [asset specificity]; without it there is no known reason for firms to exist." (Alchian, 1982, pp. 6-7, quoted by Williamson, 1985, p. 53) Asset specificity is defined as the extent to which an asset's value is dependent upon a specific customer or supplier relationship, a contract, or a product, so that part of that asset's value would be lost if the relationship, contract or product to which the asset is devoted were terminated.

Thus, asset specificity binds a collection of assets together in a firm and gives that complementary collection a reason to continue as such. Without asset specificity, an asset is worth no more to its present holder than to anyone else, so it is constantly on the market. The firm has no reason to hold and use assets rather than sell them. The claim that asset specificity is a key to the firm's existence, or at least its continuation, seems easy to defend, and it is important to accounting. The greater the specificity of an asset, the more difficult it is to observe a market price, present or past, that reflects the unique value of the asset in the firm. (See p. 48.)

The Firm as Production Function

Since Cobb and Douglas contributed their pioneering work on the production function in 1928, many economists have explained the role of the firm as that of a converter of a set of inputs into a product. The recipe for converting inputs to a product is known as the production function. "The way in which production is in fact organized is ... in ... firms, within which economic resources are applied in the production of products for sale in more or less well-organized markets." (Buchanan, 1940, p. 13) In those days, tour packages, banking services, and mutual funds were not called products. "In most of the work on the theory of the firm, it is at least implicitly assumed that the agent whose behavior is to be examined is a capitalist firm ... engaged in manufacturing, processing or perhaps extraction." (Archibald, 1987, p. 357) In much of neoclassical economics, a firm was assumed to produce a single product. Furthermore, in competitive equilibrium, firms achieved no pure profit, although they were, of course, constantly striving for it. That quest worked through the logic of marginal analysis to find the level of output at which profit was maximized. It seems likely that few would be inclined to reject the importance of the firm's role in combining inputs to produce an output, and that suggests an important role for accounting. But probably just as few would accept that function as enough to characterize a firm.

Section Summary

Brief reviews of eight different conceptions of the firm reveal a wide range of emphases. In general, most writers have overemphasized one or a few aspects and, not surprisingly, neglected some features that are important to accounting. The contracting theme emphasizes two-party exchanges but neglects a vast range of economic events that are not in themselves contracts. The coalition/relationships view stresses the organizational aspect more than the economic aspect. It includes not only contractual, two-party exchanges but also a broader set of softer relationships such as gratuitous and "baker's dozen" (an extra cookie) behavior, loyalty, voluntary adjustments of contracts, and sacrifices to accommodate other parties to the coalitions. For example, the recent discussion at the Financial Accounting Standards Board on postemployment benefits other than pensions has brought out the tendency for some practices and expectations to be noncontractual. Some of those wealth transfers are not captured by accounting.

The view of the firm as a governance structure emphasizes integration of activities that might otherwise be organized by markets. That view is in sharp contrast to the contracting theme, as it calls attention to internal, noncontractual relationships. The notion that the firm supersedes the price mechanism is similar. Such supersession is one consequence of integration and might be considered a macro explanation of why firms exist, but accounting is a microeconomic process. A micro or firm-specific reason for creation of firms would provide a sounder basis for explaining accounting.

The management-centric approach separates management from other constituents, including owners. It suggests a management point of view in accounting, with returns to all resource providers as costs. In fact, accounting does not treat returns to owners as costs. Furthermore, firms with owner/management splits were not common during the period in which most of the practices now observed in accounting were developed.

A description of a firm as a collection of assets surely overemphasizes one element to the neglect of others. The asset specificity rationale is a serious explanation for the existence of firms, and it spotlights a major source of difficulty for accounting, but its relationship to firm accounting is limited. The production function aspect emphasizes the combining of resources to make a product, which ties to product cost accounting, but it fits best in a one-product firm or in one activity of a modern integrated, diversified firm.

All of the narrow views of the firm have been found wanting. The firms in which accounting developed had broader portfolios of features.

THE FIRM

This section includes a proposed view of the nature of those firms in which accounting was developed substantially to its present state. The description is presented in two parts: first, the necessary features of a firm; second, other major features that are essentially universal, even though not absolutely required. A few comments are offered on the significance of those features for the development of accounting.

> *A firm is an economic unit directed by one manager or management team that acquires resources from other units and combines them to produce one or more products that are sold to other economic units in order to create wealth. Firms are also observed to possess other features: each is unique, holds and divides resources, integrates multiple activities, and is ultimately controlled by residual equityholders.*

A firm is, above all, an economic unit -- one member of the economy. It interacts with other economic units: households, other firms, governmental units, and other not-for-profit units. The firm is distinguished from a household or a factor owner by its role in combining resources to produce and sell an output. It is unlike governments and other not-for-profit units in that its constituents intend for it to create wealth. The scope of the firm is defined by the phrase "directed by one manager or management team," and the unit with that scope is the basis for the entity concept that is so important in accounting and that provides the primary criterion identifying which assets and other items to include in a set of consolidated financial statements.

The management direction feature is important to accounting in another way. The firm's accounting practices are controlled by management, subject to only modest external constraints. Thus, internal accounting practices are designed to meet management's information needs related to decision making (including control-oriented decisions). External reporting practices are tailored to serve management's interests by conveying the desired images to reportees, subject to constraints imposed by those reportees, regulators, and the events being reported.

The references to other parties as sources of inputs and receivers of outputs suggest relationships between the firm and other entities through markets. The market prices established in those transactions serve as end points, or anchors, for the entire network of accounting entries. Recognition of the two-party bargaining involved in setting those prices reminds one of the conflicts between management and those contracting parties. Also, if members of the top management team are not major owners, the interests of those two groups conflict. Those conflicts have led to an emphasis on reliability (including neutrality) in accounting.[2]

The clauses in the definition and supplementary description that refer to the holding, dividing and combining of resource inputs to produce outputs have profound implications for management accounting. They lead to the analytical ("allocation" in accounting jargon) and synthesizing procedures used by accountants to split and combine resource costs. They suggest the myriad of technology decisions that call for information on the costs of using inputs and intermediate resources flowing in and out of the many integrated activities of a firm. The number of possible combinations of management decisions approaches infinity, so each firm and activity within the firm is unique. Those unique firm activities employ many unique intermediate resources and produce unique outputs, thus making observation of market prices for those intermediate inputs and outputs impossible; they are not traded in markets. This leads to the proposition that accounting measurements guide the "visible hand" of management (Chandler, 1977) in internal decisions just as market prices guide the invisible hand in relationships between firms (Staubus, 1988, pp. 245-253). One could argue that the large, integrated firm and a socialist economy have one common feature; both are handicapped by the absence of competitive market prices to guide the decisions of managers of producing units that are parts of the larger entity (firm or socialist economy). Few (outside east Asia) now doubt the severity of that handicap to socialist economies. A perhaps less widely accepted hypothesis is that the absence of competitive market prices to guide the decisions of managers of activities within integrated firms handicaps those firms enough to constrain their growth by integration. (Cf. Coase, 1937, pp. 394-397; Robinson, 1931, p. 44; Kaldor, 1934, p. 68.)

The above definition of the firm includes an objective statement -- "in order to create wealth" -- that provides both an explanation for its formation and continuation and an intermediate objective for accounting. Individuals seek wealth. Any information service that reports on the firm's wealth-creating activities is bound to be of interest to its constituents. To them, the firm's success on the wealth-creation criterion potentially affects their own wealth, in varying degrees, because they have better prospects for enjoying favorable outcomes dealing with a profitable firm than dealing with an unprofitable one.[3] Accounting measures that success. That objective also implies ongoing operations and a prospective view -- rather than a process of liquidation -- which is consistent with the "going concern" (continuity) assumption in accounting. It also implies holding wealth items, which accountants call assets, and to which they devote a great deal of attention.

The final feature of the firm is the residual interest. The party who accepts the major risk-bearing responsibility has more influence over firm policies, thus giving it more opportunity to protect its most vulnerable interest against the ravages of uncertainty and conflicts of interests. That residual interest has a unique position in accounting; uncertainty makes it the unknown in the accounting equation, so much of the accounting activity is devoted to solving for it. Firm accounting reflects the residual equity, or proprietary, point of view. The return to that constituency is the only one that is not treated as a cost.

INFLUENCES OF THE FIRM'S NATURE ON THE DEVELOPMENT OF ACCOUNTING IN FIRMS: NINE PROPOSITIONS

1. *Firm accounting practices are influenced substantially by the nature of the firm.*

2. *The scope of a set of accounts and financial statements is the affairs of an entity under the direction and control of one management team.*

3. *Because the activities of the firm are the primary determinants of its accounting system, and because each firm is unique, accounting systems vary across firms.*

4. *Management's objectives for a firm's accounting are (1) to serve the information needs of the management in its quest for entity wealth, and (2) to report management's view of the success of that quest to other parties with interests in the firm and with the legal or economic power to persuade management to report to them.*

5. *Because management controls a firm's accounting, subject to modest constraints, any conflict of interest between management and another constituent group can lead to a promanagement bias in any accounting information provided to that constituency by "the firm."*

> *Recognition of that potential has led those concerned with financial reporting to emphasize reliability (including neutrality).*

6. *Constituents' interest in the firm's wealth-creating activities presents accounting with its central challenge: measurement of wealth and the amount of wealth created in a period.*

7. *The wealth creation objective has required that accounting take a prospective view consistent with continuity of the firm, rather than liquidation, in the absence of evidence to the contrary.*

8. *Because the residual equity of owners bears the net results of the firm's wealth-creating endeavors, it is a sensitive indicator of firm success; therefore, all constituents are interested in financial statements reflecting the proprietary view.*

9. *The firm's (a) wealth creation objective, (b) operational focus on resources, and (c) control by residual equity holders have led to general acceptance of a simple characterization of a firm's financial position: assets less liabilities equal owners' equity.*

CONCLUSION

The value of firm accounting depends, in part, on accountants' recognition of the fundamental features of firms. That recognition makes certain generally accepted "principles" of firm accounting -- e.g., the entity focus, the continuity assumption, the proprietary point of view -- more understandable and supportable. More importantly, it calls attention to some features that accountants tend to neglect: the interest, role, and power of management in developing accounting standards; the general interest in wealth measurement; and the uniqueness of each firm's activities and wealth items.

Certain of the above propositions have a partially hypothetical character;   further examination is appropriate. Also, many other propositions have been formulated regarding the influence of firm characteristics on the development of accounting in firms. They appear in subsequent chapters. The intent of this chapter is to stimulate interest in the dependence of firm accounting practices on the basic nature of the firm. A good understanding of that relationship may lead to better understanding of firm accounting as it exists.

NOTES

1. The consensus among historians is that the oldest surviving double-entry record is that of the government of the city of Genoa, so this premise may not be accepted by everyone. Nevertheless, the sum of all evidence is believed to support the premise as stated.

2. For more on the influence of conflicts of interests, see Chapter 4.

3. Individuals' preference for association with a profitable firm may be explained in terms of "rent-seeking behavior," (Buchanan, 1980, pp. 3-15) meaning attempts to obtain a return greater than that available in the next best use of the resource one is selling.

CHAPTER 2
TIER I INFLUENCES

In this chapter, six psychological and economic phenomena that are believed to underlie other determinants of the development of firms and of the accounting function in firms are reviewed. They are: bounded rationality, the prevalence of self-interested (opportunistic) behavior, firm uniqueness, externalities and dilution of cost/benefit consequences, information losses in transmission, and indivisibilities and economies of scale in acquisition of resources. In each case, I seek an understanding of how the phenomenon influenced the development of accounting. Loose relationships between these six and other influences are illustrated in EXHIBIT I, page 149.

BOUNDED RATIONALITY

The concept of bounded rationality was developed by Simon as a response to the classical economics assumption that economic man maximizes utility, if he is a consumer, or profit, if he is an entrepreneur. (1957, p. 196) The "principle of bounded rationality" is:

> The capacity of the human mind for formulating and solving complex problems is very small compared with the size of the problems whose solution is required for objectively rational behavior in the real world -- or even for a reasonable approximation to such objective rationality. (p. 198)
> For the first consequence of the principle of bounded rationality is that the intended rationality of an actor requires him to construct

a simplified model of the real situation in order
to deal with it. He behaves rationally with
respect to this model, and such behavior is not
even approximately optimal with respect to the
real world. (p. 199)[1]

Marschak and Radner recognized this point in their
Economic Theory of Teams: "The capacity of men to transmit
and receive information is limited even when enlarged by
mechanical communication devices .... [C]ertain information
structures are not feasible (or can be said to be infinitely
costly)." (1972, p. 129)

The principle of bounded rationality has profound
implications for the organization and management of firms and
for the development of accounting in firms. First, one observes
that actors seek to stretch or loosen the bounds on their rational
behavior. For example, they construct a simplified model of the
problem; they divide the problem into parts; they record their
progress toward its solution;   they share the task with
colleagues. Furthermore, specialists are employed to work on
certain aspects of the problem, e.g., marketing, engineering,
finance. Information is purchased from specialized purveyors;
consultants are employed.   Of particular relevance to
accounting, users accept approximations and summaries of
relevant data.   The best example of this is reliance on one
number to reflect a mass of data, e.g., unit cost, divisional
profit. More generally, accounting systems augment the limited
capacity of the human mind, and the set of minds possessed by
a firm's management team, by recording (thus removing human
memory as a constraint), classifying, summarizing, and
reporting financial information. With "unbounded rationality"
firm managements would not find accounting systems (in the
customary sense) worthwhile.

10.   *Bounded rationality has led to the development of*
        accounting systems that augment the limited capacity of
        the human mind by identifying, quantifying, classifying,

> *recording, summarizing and reporting to management and others the effects of selected economic events on the firm's wealth.*
>
> *11.* *Bounded rationality has led to the use of a materiality screen to keep the quantity of financial data reported to users within bounds; financial reports do not show details that are unlikely to affect users' judgments.*

SELF-INTEREST/OPPORTUNISM

This is not the place to delve into psychological views of the instinct for self-preservation. Instead, Georgescu-Roegen's conclusion is accepted: "[I]n all societies the typical individual continually pursues ... the increase of that [which] he can claim as his." (1971, p. 320) Again, "The first theorem (of economics) says that individuals act so as to further their own interest, even when acting as members of a group." (Alchian, 1958, p. 352) In other words, individuals looking out for themselves sometimes engage in opportunistic behavior that is contrary to the interests of others.

Attention to opportunism is not new to modern economic literature. Marshall (1895) warned that absentee owners must guard against managers taking kickbacks, shirking, and engaging in nepotism (p. 383) and addressed the issue of monitoring costs in large organizations (p. 365). More currently, Williamson defined opportunism as "self-interest seeking with guile" (1985, p. 47) including, in the language of insurance, both adverse selection (ex ante) and moral hazard (ex post). Shirking, malingering, malfeasance, excessive consumption of perquisites, and free riding are other terms for specific types of opportunistic behavior. "A healthy regard for opportunism is essential to an understanding of the purposes served by complex modes of economic organization." (Williamson, p. 388)

Recognition of the hazards of opportunism has led managers to develop techniques for controlling, counteracting, or channelling such behavior in the interests of the organization. Williamson (p. 48) recommends that one seek "credible commitments" from other contracting parties, rather than rely on good faith or legal remedies. Conventional control-oriented techniques such as "internal check," auditing, bonding, and double-entry accounting address opportunism. A more positive approach aims at motivating people to work toward the objectives of the organization. Examples are planning and control schemes that rely heavily on accounting, performance reporting in general (e.g., "responsibility accounting"), and incentive compensation plans.

The tendency of self-interest to extend to a greater entity, through feelings of fraternal loyalty, is an additional factor to be considered. People tend to build a biased view of the qualities possessed by the department, division, firm, school, political subdivision, or nation to which they "belong." Success for that entity tends to "rub off" on the individual. Such a bias is widely recognized in accounting and auditing, and that recognition has influenced their development.

12. *The prevalence of opportunistic and self-interested behavior leads to incorporation of control features within accounting systems, including double entry, performance reporting, auditing, and various internal check features.*
13. *The self-interest of persons in firms can lead to bias in financial reporting, so neutrality and verifiability are prized qualities of financial information.*

FIRM UNIQUENESS

In classical and neoclassical economics, an industry consisted of one to many firms producing the same product(s) from the same factor inputs. Firms in an industry varied in size and in efficiency, but otherwise were similar. More recently, both the comparability of firms and economists' perceptions of the similarities and differences among firms have changed.

To be exact, every firm is unique -- no two are precisely alike in all details. Foregoing precision, one could argue that firms A and B in the same industry, say wheat farming or convenience stores, are essentially identical. In general, however, firms differ with respect to size, organization structure, location, products, financial structure, activities, portfolios of assets and liabilities, and so on. Resource inputs tend to differ with respect to quality, location and so on. Product outputs of a firm differ in some respects from those of seemingly similar firms. Many of a firm's intermediates (resources at the point of use (after acquisition) and internally transferred commodities and services) are unique in place and in resource relationships. Use of "flexible manufacturing systems" controlled by sophisticated software permits manufacturing firms quickly to vary their product assortments, and the continual development of new "products" in service industries permits all to claim uniqueness. Unique goods are difficult for prospective buyers, and to a lesser extent sellers, to evaluate, a subject that has been addressed informatively by Akerlof (1970) and Barzel (1982) among others. Uniqueness adds to transaction costs, so contributes to integration of activities in lieu of transacting in markets.

An important implication of firm uniqueness is that observed market prices set in transactions between other economic units do not price the setting-specific resources acquired and consumed by a firm, the intermediates transferred within it, and its completed products on hand. "Market simulation accounting" (Staubus, 1985, 1986) has evolved to meet the demand in integrated firms for measurements of those setting-specific assets and liabilities. Market simulation accounting means the selection and blending of pertinent observed market prices and other evidence in accordance with accepted principles of market economics to assess the price at which an asset or liability would trade in an active market

(1986, p. 118). Increasing uniqueness of firms may require accounting to adapt further and faster to fulfill its responsibility for measuring those items and providing value information to managers. Furthermore, unique features of firms might be expected to lead to unique accounting systems aimed at the planning-control-performance reporting functions. If each firm consists of a unique set of activities, and if firm accounting systems develop to meet the needs of the firm, it follows that each firm has a unique accounting system.

14. *The activities of the firm are the primary determinants of its accounting system; each firm is unique, so accounting systems vary across firms.*

15. *"Market simulation accounting" has evolved to meet the demand in integrated firms for measurements of their unique assets and liabilities.*

EXTERNALITIES

In his seminal Economics of Welfare (1920), Pigou developed the notion of "investments in which ... marginal private net product is greater than marginal social net product." (p. 185) That notion included costs borne by parties other than the one carrying out the action in question, for example, air pollution. In the current literature of economics, an "externality" is a cost (negative externality) or benefit (positive externality) falling on, and absorbed by, someone external to the firm or other unit taking an action. They may be called "firm externalities" in the present context. (For a technical definition, see Laffont in Palgrave (1987, Vol. 2, p. 263).) The failure of accounting to deal with firm externalities, activity (e.g., department) externalities, and individual externalities -- more generally "economic unit externalities" -- and accounting's successes and failures in dealing with "period externalities" are argued in this section.

Matching: An Economics and Accounting Concept

Economic behavior means acting on the basis of an economic analysis -- a comparison of the prospective costs and benefits of the action. The costs and benefits taken into consideration are those that fall on the decision maker. If one takes an action that he/she perceives not to be in his/her own interest it is either altruistic or forced action, not economic action. Some would say that altruistic and forced action are economic behavior in that they are aimed at maximizing the actor's long-run utility given the circumstances. If so, the cost-benefit approach may be thought of as the economic view of all behavior. Or, "economic" may be synonymous with rational, or analytical.

Given bounded rationality and self-interested behavior of actors, the costs and benefits taken into consideration are not likely to be all inclusive. In addition to the perception screen that filters out the unknown, the self-interest screen imposes a scope limitation. A decision-maker's cost-benefit analysis includes only those factors that impact him/her, directly or through the economic unit for which he/she is responsible, e.g., the firm. The factors excluded on the basis of incidence are called externalities.

The most general rule of economic behavior is: take all actions that increase wealth. The first example learned by many economics students is the rule for optimizing the level of output: adjust the rate of output towards that rate at which marginal revenue equals marginal cost. The finance and accounting student learns the net present value rule for making capital investments. Economic actions are intended to increase profit -- the flow view -- or wealth -- the stocks view.

Economic behavior means comparing, and netting, the favorable and unfavorable effects (advantages and disadvantages) of a possible action. Likewise, in the accounting process, the favorable and unfavorable effects of sets of actions are compared and netted. The language of accounting is replete with terms connoting two: matching, exchanges, transactions, and double entry. The various forms of an accounting equation -- balance sheet, income statement, account -- emphasize comparisons of inflows and outflows. Accounting is the systematic calculation form of economic analysis, with emphasis on an ex post view of the set of events affecting a defined entity during a specified period. Identifying and comparing favorable and unfavorable effects of actions are the essence of economic behavior and of the accounting process.

Types of Externalities

Externalities are anomalies in economic analysis and accounting in that they are not "properly" matched. When actors do not bear, feel, and base their actions on all social costs and benefits, markets are prevented from achieving Pareto efficient allocations. Unpriced positive or negative externalities are social inefficiencies. This is an economist's view of what are called "firm externalities" in this paper. Externalities are costs or benefits that are ignored by a given actor but are recognized, and viewed as significant, by observers outside the economic unit producing them. The broader the economic unit, the fewer the externalities. Consider a sovereign nation. Its actions affecting the seas, the atmosphere, global war, highly contagious diseases, and a few others are significant to other nations, but most of its actions are of only minor import to other nations. Looking at a domestic firm, any of the above effects, plus a number of extra-firm costs and benefits affecting the domestic economy may be viewed as externalities. Firm segments, such as divisions, departments, and narrow activities, may impose many externalities on other units within the firm and may bear externalities exported by other firm activities. These may be called "activity externalities." At the finest level of analysis, an individual in a firm may not bear all of the costs, or enjoy all of the benefits of his/her actions, thus creating "individual externalities." The narrower the economic unit under analysis, the relatively greater are the externalities from its actions -- and the greater the measurement error due to externalities. This tendency is important to top managers concerned with the design of governance structures in large firms.

From the point of view of any economic unit, it may transfer to others (export) both favorable and unfavorable one-way effects and may receive from others both favorable and unfavorable effects. An externalities accounting system would disclose a favorable or unfavorable "balance of trade" for the entity. Unfortunately, the two concepts -- externalities and accounting -- are almost incompatible, because the former tend to be unmeasurable.

Activity and individual externalities are familiar to those who have spent a lot of time in large organizations. Argyris (1953) used the term "department centeredness" for the tendency of personnel in a given department to engage in selfish behavior at the expense of other departments. Thus, with sequential operations on a product, the first department may make the transferee department wait for batches of product that are convenient for the transferor department to pass on, or it may pass on product in a loose pile instead of a neat stack, or so dirty that it must be cleaned by the transferee department.

Turning to individual externalities, "incentive dilution" refers to the spreading of a cost or benefit over parties in the organization other than the one directly affected by the related benefit or cost. A good example is a perquisite enjoyed by one partner in a professional firm that is paid for by all of the profit-sharing partners. From the first partner's point of view, the cost is diluted. In general, whenever less than 100 per cent of the costs or benefits of an action, as viewed from a wider perspective, fall on the decision maker, cost-benefit matching and the related decision making suffers, according to the wider perspective. "Free riders" enjoy benefits paid for by someone else. Shirkers do not carry their share of the load. The most socially beneficial cost-benefit matching and decision making, according to this view, is likely to be achieved by individuals working in one-person economic units. They tend to bear one hundred percent of the costs and benefits of their efforts in the absence of externalities. The worst decisions are by workers on fixed salaries in a major collectivized economy; they tend to receive zero per cent of the benefits of their incremental efforts and bear close to zero per cent of the costs of their decisions.

An example of poor cost-benefit matching that is familiar to academics is found in a taxpayer-supported university. The students and faculty favor "better" (usually more expensive) education while taxpayers lean towards more economical operations. With the product's price (tuition) set unilaterally instead of in markets, the demand for education (or at least degrees) typically exceeds the supply. Rationing is administered by the admissions office.

Now consider the development of accounting long ago in the first firm with absentee owners and hired managers. Suppose that the firm is relying on cash basis accounting and that the managers foresee short tenure unless they show good results. Their narrow focus on the firm suggests that they are not concerned about any positive or negative externalities they may produce. Their myopia leads them to count a bird in the hand as worth two in the bush; positive payoffs to the firm in future periods are severely discounted and negative payoffs in the future are of little concern. They are "period externalities." At the same time, any benefits received this period due to prior period expenditures are welcomed, while disbursements required because of predecessors' commitments are cursed. They are externalities exported by the previous management and imported to this period. Under the assumption that the firm's management changes each period, each period is like a separate firm that can export or import positive or negative externalities. This scenario sets the stage for accrual-deferral accounting.

In their basic accounting meanings, to accrue is to record as affecting income in a period prior to a cash movement; to defer is to record as affecting income in a period subsequent to a cash movement. Thus, when the practice of *accruing* revenues and receivables is imposed on a cash basis accounting system, a "period," thought of as a firm, loses the positive externality contributed by the "previous period" and gains credit for the positive externality contributed to subsequent periods. When expenses and liabilities are accrued, the period is freed of the burden of obligations incurred by the previous period, and accepts responsibility for its own obligations that have not yet been paid. Similarly, the *deferral* of costs gives a period credit for the positive externalities it contributes to subsequent periods, e.g., ending inventory, while charging the current period for the positive externalities received from previous periods, e.g., beginning inventory. Deferral of revenues charges the current period for obligations it imposes on subsequent periods and credits it for obligations imposed on it by prior periods. Accrual-deferral accounting accounts for (internalizes) period externalities, thereby removing management's myopia. A period is no longer an economic unit. Cross-period effects are no longer ignored as externalities.

Accounting for Externalities

Going back to the concept of economic behavior as taking actions on the basis of cost-benefit analyses, one might ask: "How does accounting contribute to economic behavior?" To successful economic behavior? Accounting should not be expected to change people's underlying motivations, or intentions, but it may serve them by helping them achieve their objectives. Which benefits and costs do actors intend to consider? Which would they like to consider? In practice, there probably is not a strict cut-off. People give some consideration, in many cases, to disutility inflicted on their neighbors, at least if they are friendly neighbors. But we do not quantify as a personal cost the disutility we inflict on a neighbor. The calculus of costs and benefits usually is limited to prices set in exchanges in which we participate -- our purchases, our sales -- but occasionally including surrogates for such prices, such as the estimated price we would have had to pay for a nonmonetary benefit we receive, e.g., health insurance. If the actors do not quantify externalities, accounting cannot record them. Accountants do not account for matters that people "ought to" consider but in fact do not fully weigh as they compare costs and benefits of prospective actions.

Now consider firms. Accounting means to take into account, i.e., to include in the calculus. In the present cost-benefit context, a firm does not bear the pain and suffering inflicted on other economic units, unless it is explicitly made to do so, as by fines or assessments. If the firm bears no cost, its accountant can record no cost. If the firm contributes positive externalities to others, by definition it receives no credit, so there is nothing to record. Imported externalities -- positive externalities received and negative ones borne -- affect the firm's accounts, but they are not recorded separately because of difficulties in recognizing and measuring them and because there is little incentive to do so. In general, firm externalities are not recognized in accounting. Market exchanges are quantified by the actors and recorded by accounting. Externalities are "extra-market," one-way transfers of costs or benefits. Because a firm's exported externalities are not borne or enjoyed by the firm, accounting's omission is not a failure in the context of the firm's interests. From the social point of view, however, economic unit externalities are accounting failures.

This leaves intra-firm externalities -- activity and individual -- as possible subjects to be dealt with by accounting. Visualize an organizational structure that includes various activities, each under the direction of a manager, and with an activity accounting system that reports on the success of each activity. The typical product division structure with transfers across divisions at adjusted market prices is a large scale version of such an environment. To what extent do interactivity externalities enter the accounting system? If transfer prices are set strictly on the basis of observed market prices, the answer is: not at all, because externalities, by definition, are not reflected in market prices.

Now divide the set of possible externalities into two subsets: externalities affecting trading partners and those affecting third parties. Effects on trading partners can be internalized in the price when the trades are genuine market transactions. If your product is packaged in a way that makes its handling risky for my workers, I will insist on taking that into consideration in setting the price I am willing to pay for the product. But if I manage a transferee activity within a firm and we are not free to negotiate a price in the presence of external alternatives, I may get stuck with a negative externality -- a cost that is not reflected in the administered (e.g., cost-based) transfer price. The nature of that externality may be such that it costs my activity an incremental two dollars per unit of product while you -- the transferor -- could have remedied the problem at a cost of $1.50. This offers a role for administered pricing of the "externality," viz. a charge of two dollars per unit to the transferor in the form of a reduction in the transfer price of the commodity, thus giving the activity with the power to remedy the safety problem an incentive to do so. This may seem, at first glance, to be a type of imposed solution that is not likely to be efficient, but actually it is a nonmarket imposition on a nonmarket relationship -- an attempt to offset an error created by lack of a market price for the transfer. Thus, given that all internal transfers involve unique assets for which no market price is observable so market simulation accounting (Staubus, 1985) must be applied, it can be applied so as to take into account any positive or negative pseudo-externalities that accompany the transfer. Then the favorable or unfavorable "side effects" are converted from unaccountable externalities to accountable internalities.

Another possible type of activity externality is the positive or negative side effect of one activity on a third party activity -- a bystander. For example, one activity may impose noise pollution on its neighbors within the plant. This type of problem is most likely to be resolved, if at all, by administrative direction rather than by a monetary penalty-reward system, just as it is when the neighbors are separate economic units and the direction comes from a governmental authority. Again, there is no explicit accounting for the externality. "Externality" is synonymous with "accounting failure" in this context.

Individuals working in firms typically are not represented by unique accounts, in contrast to the representation of departments. Individual externalities, therefore, are rarely recognized in accounting. If an individual contributes positively or negatively to his/her colleagues' work, that is recognized, if at all, administratively, as in personnel evaluations. The phenomenon labelled "incentive dilution" in an earlier paragraph has negative effects on efficiency because of a failure to match costs and benefits -- a person's efforts and results -- in the sense that the individual does not bear both in full measure. Accounting mirrors economic reality with its "matching failure."

The usual impacts on a set of financial statements of several common classes of transactions and externalities are depicted in the accompanying chart.

16.   *The tendency of economic activities to produce period externalities has contributed to the practice of accrual-deferral accounting, which effectively internalizes those phenomena.*

17.   *Many period externalities that are not readily measurable, i.e., intangible liabilities and assets, are not accrued or deferred; those failures limit the value and tarnish the image of accounting.*

18.   *Firm externalities are omitted from accounts unless they affect firm wealth, i.e., are internalized.*

19.   *The value to decision makers and society of cost-benefit matching has favorably influenced the standing of accounting as a valuable service.*

20.   *Accounting measures and reports on internalities -- the costs and benefits that actors match with their actions.*

TRANSACTIONS, EXTERNALITIES, ACCOUNTING AND NONACCOUNTING

	Events of Earlier Periods	Events of the Accounting Period	Events of Later Periods
Other parties	e	a 1 b	f
The firm	2	Domain of a Set of Financial Statements	3
	c		d

Note: Transactions are denoted by numbers, externalities by letters.

1. Recorded transactions involving exchanges.
2. Deferrals recognized in accounting, i.e., receipts and expenditures recognized as affecting income in a later period(s).
3. Accruals recognized in accounting, i.e., receipts and expenditures recognized as affecting income in an earlier period(s).
a,b. Externalities imported by the firm (a) and exported by the firm (b) during the accounting period, i.e., "unrecognized" costs or benefits.
c,d. Interperiod, intrafirm costs/benefits not "recognized" by accounting as accruals or deferrals, e.g., investments in off-balance sheet assets or incurring ill will.
e,f. Possible interperiod, interparty externalities.

INFORMATION LOSSES IN TRANSMISSION

> There is a great deal of evidence that almost all organizational structures tend to produce false images in the decision maker, and that the larger and more authoritarian the organization, the better the chance that its top decision makers will be operating in purely imaginary worlds. This perhaps is the most fundamental reason for supposing that there are ultimately diminishing returns to scale. (Boulding, 1968, p. 8)

Frustrations with internal communications in large organizations are familiar to many. The concern here is with the transmission of information that has reached one part of the organization to other parts that can use it. This problem is not addressed by such abstract neoclassical models as that of perfect competition, where perfect knowledge is assumed. Recognition of bounded rationality, however, leads to recognition that people cannot transmit or receive information without errors of commission and omission. Given the self-interest of the individuals involved, one must also consider the possibility that information is modified, consciously or subconsciously, by people through whom it passes. Cost is also a limitation on communications within firms, including the cost of excessive communication, e.g., "copying" too many people.

Three specific factors may be identified as contributing to information loss. One is the phenomenon of loss of information through serial reproduction. A familiar demonstration of that loss is the children's whispering game, "pass it on," in which the first person whispers a message to the second who, in turn, whispers it to the third, and so on. Children are amused by the subsequent comparison of the original message with the one reported by the last child in the line. That phenomenon has been studied by Bartlett in various oral, written, and line drawing forms, with the result that:

It is now perfectly clear that serial reproduction normally brings about startling and radical alterations in the material dealt with. Epithets are changed into their opposites; incidents and events are transposed; names and numbers rarely survive intact for more than a few reproductions; opinions and conclusions are reversed -- nearly every possible variation seems as if it can take place, even in a relatively short series. (Bartlett, 1932, p. 175, quoted by Williamson, 1970, p. 25).

The second plausible reason to believe that large organizations lose information in the transmission process is the time factor in communication through levels. In those frequent cases in which information reaches the organization through a low-level person, or originates at a low level within the organization, additional layers in the management hierarchy normally add to the time required for the word to reach the top, and for the response to return to a point of action. In certain organizations, the management process involves almost continuous sequences of directions, feedback, and redirection. Although improvements in computational and communication equipment can help, *ceteris paribus*, every additional layer through which information must pass costs time, primarily because each manager receiving information takes time to decide and act on the filtering, augmenting, and summarizing that he/she undertakes. Thus, both accuracy and speed of communication typically are impaired by increasing size of organization.

Another probable causal factor in loss of information through internal communications is the exponential growth in the number of possible one-to-one relationships as the number of people in an organization increases. If a person receiving various bits of information from outside the firm is to pass each bit on to the in-firm person in the best position to use it, without going through the hierarchy (and incurring that set of costs), that first person must identify the proper person to contact and make that contact. In practice, the mix of direct methods, use of the hierarchy, and neglecting to pass the information on at all must vary a great deal, but all are costly. Again, developments in data processing are helpful.

Accounting systems are firms' response to information losses as described above. The emphasis is on the systematic feature of accounting. The value of systematic accounting, including the most fundamental feature -- double-entry -- as well as such seldom-appreciated internal control features as receipts and other printed forms with serial numbers and carbon copies, and various software controls, is generally recognized. For example, auditors consider unrecorded assets to be more vulnerable to loss than assets on which information is systematically recorded, because information on the unrecorded asset is at risk, e.g., known only to one opportunistic individual.

21.   *Firms respond to the tendency for information to be lost in intra-firm transmission by installing double-entry accounting systems accompanied by such information control devices as printed forms, software controls, and internal auditing.*

INDIVISIBILITIES AND ECONOMIES OF SCALE IN ACQUISITION OF RESOURCES

The phenomena of interest here are acquisitions of resources in large packages at low unit costs compared with alternative acquisition practices. Several examples may clarify the point: (1) Specialist labor services -- for example, those of an office equipment repair person or a patent attorney -- may be acquired via a full-time employee or by the job or hour as needed. (2) High-capacity, long-lived automatic equipment may replace several manually operated machines and their hourly-paid operators. (3) A large, efficiently laid out plant may substitute for two smaller, less efficient ones. (4) National, mass-media advertising may replace a set of local advertising plans. (5) Purchase of the lifetime services of an asset may substitute for renting its services for short periods. In all of these cases, the firm may be able to acquire services at lower unit costs by contracting for the larger quantities, and may also save on transaction costs.

Accounting for large packages of resources by spreading their costs over accounting periods on a time basis has led accountants to the "fixed cost" interpretation. In accounting jargon, a fixed cost is an operating cost that does not change in the "short run" because of small or moderate changes in the volume of operations. A stream of services is provided or offered by the asset, and those services are either utilized or lost. If the stream of services can be either consumed or turned off and stored, the cost is not fixed, as in the case of equipment that depreciates only as used, so might be accounted for as a variable cost by the units-of-production depreciation method. Even in cases in which the asset's service potential declines with time, market evidence generally does not support a straight-line decline in value. Many "fixed costs" are accounting constructs.

An interrelated set of accounting developments has grown out of the fixed-variable distinction: break-even analysis, flexible budgeting and the associated volume variance; direct, marginal, or variable costing; and contribution margin analysis. To some extent, these accounting techniques have achieved more acceptance during periods of low business activity and the accompanying idle capacity -- such as the 1930s (Harris, 1936) -- than in periods of fuller utilization of capacity. The fixed costs of plant capacity are viewed by many as excludible from production costs, but others disagree. The controversy remains unresolved. Some view the conventional accounting interpretation of fixed costs and the accounting techniques built upon it as a crude response to the phenomenon in question. (Kaplan, 1986, p. 138; Staubus, 1988, pp. 219-224).

Another angle from which to view the "fixed cost" interpretation of accounting for costs of indivisible assets is the cost-data-for-pricing view. Two sets of evidence are available. The "full costers" report that most manufacturing firms rely heavily on product cost numbers that include fixed costs (Govindarajan and Anthony, 1983). The "marginal costers" see a great deal of less-than-full-cost pricing, e.g., in airlines, hotels, restaurants, and bidding for work under idle capacity conditions. But one does not see descriptions of double entry accounting systems that yield marginal cost numbers over a wide range of volume and for various time horizons. This leads to the observation that accounting has not yet devised cost accounting concepts and systematic procedures that produce cost data relevant to pricing decisions in a variety of circumstances. "Extra-system" costing plays a significant role.

Another "extra-system" type of accounting that may be viewed as resulting from indivisibilities is the discounted cash flow analysis techniques that are used in investment project analysis. Indivisibilities in acquisitions, together with nonredeployability, results in large dollar-year commitments in which the cost of capital is material. DCF techniques put cost of capital into capital expenditures planning.

22. *No consensus has been achieved on systematic accounting for large-package assets, so ad hoc analytical techniques flourish.*
23. *Resources acquired in large packages not divisible into smaller, uniform, physical units often are accounted for entirely on a time basis due to the complexity, cost, and other disadvantages of more refined market simulation accounting as viewed by managers.*
24. *Costs of using services acquired in large packages are not spread in a straight-line time pattern because they are fixed costs; they are interpreted as fixed costs because accountants spread them in a straight-line*

pattern.   An accounting artifact is treated as an economic phenomenon.

NOTE

1.   Whether Simon's insight was inspired by one of his University of Chicago mentors is an issue for conjecture. Those who recall Frank Knight's oral expressions of disdain for "an irrational passion for dispassionate rationality" and his doubt that economists were paying attention to the "kinds of people that I know" might see his influence on Simon.

CHAPTER 3
TIER II INFLUENCES

The influences on the development of firms and firm accounting that are reviewed in this chapter are seen as growing out of the considerations discussed in chapters 1 and 2. They are cost of information, asset uniqueness and performance evaluation and incentive plans. Along with conflicts of interests -- an influence so extensive it deserves its own chapter (4), they are placed in Tier II in EXHIBIT I, page 149.

COST OF INFORMATION

"Information costs are the costs of transportation from ignorance to omniscience, and seldom can a trader afford to take the entire trip." (Stigler, 1967, p. 291) Taking into account the cost of information in relation to accounting is not a new phenomenon. It was an understated and natural feature of the environment at the London School of Economics and Political Science (LSE) in the 1930s when and where so much progress was made on economic measurement concepts. Prominent among the contributors to that work were Hicks, Kaldor, Plant, Robbins, and, a little later, Baxter, Coase, Edwards, Lerner, Solomons, and Thirlby. Which of them were accountants and which economists is neither clear nor important, for the accountants knew their economics, and the economists were interested in applied issues.

Coase's writings include consideration of the cost of information in specific situations. After explaining to his accountant readers "that it will pay to expand production so long as marginal revenue is expected to be greater than marginal cost and the avoidable costs of the total output less than the total receipts," Coase went on to suggest: "It would be Utopian to imagine that a business man, except by luck, could manage to attain this position of maximum profit. Indeed, it may cost more to discover this point than the additional profits that would be earned." (1938, pp. 110-111) Again, on p. 146: "It may, of course, often be the case that a precise calculation of the avoidable costs of a particular decision would be too expensive and that therefore a procedure is adopted which gives a figure that can only be regarded as an approximation to avoidable costs." Then came the principle:

> What seems to me important, however, is that the significance of the cost figure one is trying to calculate should be understood and that the reason for adopting a method which does not precisely measure avoidable costs should be that the revenue lost through the inaccuracy of the method is smaller than the probable expense of obtaining more exact information.

Edwards emphasized the principle that information is an economic good in a style that was natural (to the point of including a terminological flaw) for business-oriented scholars: "Costing fails in its object unless it adds more to net profit than the expense of running the system" (1937, p. 278). He elaborated as follows: "In general, then, our method of attack will have to be: firstly to decide what information we should regard as necessary, if its collection were costless, and secondly to consider whether this information is of sufficient importance to warrant the expense of its collection." (p. 279) The point is not to attribute the idea of comparing the cost and value of information to Coase and/or Edwards,[1] but rather to conjecture that the idea was taken for granted by members of the LSE school of economic accounting thought in the 1930s. Outside of academia, its instinctive recognition by economizing managers and accountants might have influenced the development of accounting practices, e.g., regarding degree of precision, amount of detail, and frequency of reporting, especially in management accounting. The costs of loosening the bounds of ignorance have always influenced the behavior of economic actors.

25. *An accounting choice is an economic decision, so choices of accounting methods are based on cost-benefit reasoning, thus limiting the complexity, fineness, and scope of the accounting systems developed in firms.*

26. *Cost of accounting was an influential factor in acceptance of specific accounting practices such as treating interest as a period expense, measurement of most nonmonetary assets at historical costs, the three-cost-elements and broad overhead pools conventions in product costing, the stable monetary unit assumption, and the materiality doctrine.*

ASSET UNIQUENESS

Our interest here is in the tendency for a firm's assets to differ from those of any other firm, despite nominal similarities. Uniqueness encompasses asset specificity, nonredeployability, setting specificity, and complementarity, all of which are discussed in this subsection. Without these characteristics, asset accounting would be as easy, and as successful, as accounting for securities traded in an active market. Their influence on accounting has been immense. Firm uniqueness and indivisibilities are the most obvious Tier I influences providing bases for uniqueness, but asset specificity can also be tied to opportunistic behavior. The explanation of firm uniqueness in Chapter 2 leads to the conclusion that nearly all of the assets and liabilities of a firm have unique combinations of features, with the differences ranging from minor to major.

Asset specificity and nonredeployability

Another approach to the uniqueness of assets works through the economic concepts of asset specificity and nonredeployability. An asset's specificity is the extent to which its value is dependent on a specific customer or supplier relationship or contract, so a loss would be incurred if that relationship or contract were terminated. The assets of concern here are investments made in support of specific relationships; they may be interfirm or intrafirm relationships. Williamson (1985, p. 55) identifies four types of asset specificity: (1) site specificity, i.e., the location of immobile assets; (2) physical specificity, as when a supplier invests in specialized dies for making a part required by one customer; (3) human assets involving investments in know-how or relationships; and (4) dedicated assets, such as service equipment kept at a customer's location for servicing a manufacturer's products at that location. To this set, David Teece (1988) might add intellectual property, if it is not included in (3) and (4) above. Masten et al. (1991, pp. 10-11) suggest adding temporal specificity; the value of a stock of services to a customer may depend heavily on the timing of its availability from a supplier, and its value to the supplier depends on the timing of a customer's demand. Other economists have emphasized similar concepts and terms. Jacob Marschak (1938, p. 323) wrote of the plasticity of an asset: the ease of "maneuvering into and out of various yields after the asset has been acquired" and "low variability of its price." As related to teams, Alchian and Woodward (1987, p. 113) suggested that "A resource is 'dependent' when it would lose value if separated from the team (firm)." Grossman and Hart (1986, p. 696) were concerned with "relationship specific investments."

Asset specificity plays a vital role in the economics of the firm. Greater asset specificity, i.e., relationship-specific assets, tends to be associated with higher transaction costs and lower production costs. A common example is investments in specialized equipment that can reduce total unit production costs if usable over a normal life. If the output is sold to one customer, protection of the specialized investment may require expensive contractual arrangements to assure continuation of the relationship on terms satisfactory to both parties; examples are clauses dealing with responses to inflation and to variations in volume. "The whole rationale for the employer-employee status, and even for the existence of firms, rests on (asset specificity); without it there is no known reason for firms to exist." (Alchian, 1982, pp. 6-7, quoted by Williamson, 1985, p. 53). His point is that the key reason for vertical integration, i.e., for intra-firm rather than inter-economic unit relationships among sequential activities, is to lessen the hazards of investing in relationship-specific assets (including humans) without controlling the related activity. Asset specificity often is associated with nonredeployability -- relatively low bail-out market value -- because the highly specific asset typically is tailored to serve a special relationship. It may be physically or contractually difficult to move and may serve poorly elsewhere. Thus, it has a relatively low value in any other use. In accounting terms, it has a low salvage value. In financial terms, investments in such assets are risky.

To invest in a "nonredeployable" asset is to put oneself at the mercy of the contracting party (the risk of being "held up," according to Alchian and Woodward (1988, pp. 67-68)) at the contract renewal date. The transformation of a competitive bidding commencement of a contracting relationship into one of bilateral supply thereafter, when the two parties are somewhat committed to each other, has been labeled the "fundamental transformation" by Williamson (1985, p. 61). The uniqueness of the assets associated with such relationships contrasts sharply with the fungibility of marketable securities or graded commodities traded in futures contracts.

Setting specificity

The "accounting model" of the economics of the firm shows individual assets and liabilities rather than relationships among them. No particular principle for unitizing assets has been articulated in the accounting literature. How many assets does an accountant recognize for one aircraft or one blast furnace or one assembly line? Acquisition at different dates, differences in lives, severability, and other features seem to affect accountants' treatments of asset units. In actuality, however, different items that accountants recognize as assets typically work together in contributing to the cash flows that are the ultimate product of enterprise activities. Complementarity -- the dependence of two or more resources on each other to produce an output -- clearly is an aspect of setting specificity.

Once we accept the notion that each firm is unique, it is not difficult to recognize that each firm holds assets that are unique to it, primarily because no two firms' assets are in precisely the same setting, or relationships to other resources. A particular model of machine does not offer the same prospective contribution to cash flow in firm A as it does in firm B, and only its contribution in the owning entity is part of that entity's wealth. Thus, all assets, possibly with a few exceptions that are trivial to accounting, are *setting specific.* Consequently, observable market prices do not reflect the views of buyers and sellers regarding the value of an asset in its specific setting, a condition called incomplete markets. All observable market prices are defective as measures of a firm's assets, because no observable price reflects the exchange of money for the rights to the setting-specific asset's contributions to firm cash flows.

More can be said about the unobservability of prices for unique assets. Uniqueness means that a price is never set for the asset. There is never a trade in which that unique asset is given up by a seller and acquired by a buyer. So the seller is accepting a satisfactory price for his/her unique asset and the buyer is paying a satisfactory price for the different unique asset he/she is obtaining. Nor does a price observed when a similar asset is sold by B to C reflect the value of A's unique asset.

Unique firms holding portfolios of unique assets (and liabilities) pose major challenges for accountants. Consider an easy case: an investment company holding only frequently traded securities. The practices of American "mutual funds" are familiar to many accountants. How large is the accounting staff (aside from those processing routine transactions) of even a huge mutual fund company? Very small. How much literature has been published on the accounting problems of mutual funds? Very little. Asset measurement in such firms is a trivial, but important exercise, and the results are accorded the rare compliment of heavy reliance; the firm's shares are traded at book values. Nevertheless, setting specificity is relevant to investment companies. Observers of closed end investment companies are aware of the spreads between "net asset value" and market price of the shares of those companies, suggesting that the setting-specific values of a company's assets and liabilities differ from the prices observed on the securities markets on which the components of the portfolio are traded. Setting specificity is a critical factor in explaining the differences among the values of superficially similar assets. It is much too material to be ignored by accountants. And it is not.

Accounting's response

How has accounting responded to the prevalence of asset uniqueness over the centuries during which firms and accounting have developed? In the absence of observable market prices for the setting-specific assets and liabilities of unique firms, what techniques have been developed "by accounting" to measure those wealth items for recognition in a firm's accounts? More succinctly, what is accounting's response to incomplete markets?

The general answer is: in the absence of observable market prices for setting-specific assets and liabilities, accounting attempts to simulate what those prices would be under a complete markets regime. See page 27 above for a definition of market simulation accounting.

Accounting's response to asset uniqueness may be illustrated by listing a few of the accounting procedures commonly used to measure assets and liabilities:

1.   Synthesizing the buying prices of resources used in the production of an asset, e.g., product cost accounting.
2.   Deducting from an observed price for a similar asset the prices of resources still required to convert an asset to a "saleable condition," i.e., net realizable value.
3.   Dividing an observed price into parts, i.e., analytical allocation.
4.   Deducting from an observed price (a sale by the firm) a provision for probability of failure to collect.
5.   Deducting from an observed price a price for cost of capital, i.e., discounting.
6.   Substituting an old price for a current price that is unobservable, difficult to observe, or otherwise objectionable, e.g., "historical cost." (This practice often reports a number that is not defensible as the best available simulation of a price for the setting-specific asset.)
7.   Substituting an observed buying price for a similar asset for an unobservable price for the asset's prospective contributions to firm cash flows, i.e., replacement cost.
8.   "Matrix pricing" (multiple regression) of infrequently traded securities, e.g., municipal bonds.
9.   The "equity method" of accounting for equity securities owned.

A review of a list of "market simulation accounting procedures" reveals that other aspects of firm economics, such as conflicts of interests and cost of information, have constrained the evolution of accounting's response to asset uniqueness. Interest in simulating a setting-specific market price is not the sole influence on accounting measurement.

One should also recognize that market simulation accounting for relationship-specific and otherwise specialized assets is bound to be crude at best. Consider the difference between relatively redeployable assets such as popular models of trucks and airplanes and quite nonredeployable assets such as many intellectual properties and piping systems in chemical plants. The quasi-rents (Marshall, 1895, p. 219) earned on nonredeployable assets -- a residual portion of product revenues -- may swing widely over time, and their values to other parties typically are low or setting-sensitive. Thus, any value assessment related to a firm's nonredeployable asset is likely to be volatile as well as a poor surrogate for the asset's setting-specific value. So why bother?

In general, the more unique the asset, the less satisfactory the accounting for it. Thus, accounting for securities owned, claims to cash, and graded commodities is viewed as more satisfactory than accounting for long-lived plant assets and intangible investments (including human resources and internally developed "goodwill".) An obvious effect of extreme uniqueness is great difficulty, therefore infrequency, of revaluation after acquisition, e.g., in applications of the lower-of-cost-and-market rule. Instead, arbitrary interperiod allocations of asset costs are invited, and certain ones -- especially internally developed intangibles -- are omitted from balance sheets. When unique assets are retained on balance sheets for long periods, users may have little confidence in the measurements reported, and one might expect conscientious accountants and regulators to express concern about how to measure the frequent impairments in the values of such assets. Dissatisfaction with the measurement of unique assets and the cost of using them may be reflected in confusion regarding the disposition of costs of idle capacity and sunk costs.

Based on the above reasoning, the influence of asset uniqueness on the development of accounting in firms may be condensed to six summary propositions, one of which (27) is a convenient variation of proposition 15:

27. *"Market simulation accounting" has evolved to meet the demand for measurements of unique assets.*

28. *The difficulties and weaknesses inherent in market simulation accounting for unique assets have led to the development of accounting practices that give great weight to economy of accounting, reliance on externally imposed rules, and semi-arbitrary estimates.*

29. *Difficulties in observing relevant market prices for unique nonfungible assets make use of the lower-of-cost-and-market rule costly and unreliable.*

30. *The reliability and economy of historical input prices dominate the simulation superiority of current, completed-cycle exit prices in the measurement of many unique assets.*

31. *The values of measurements of many unique assets are perceived as low by both the managements who control the measurement processes and the readers who use the results.*

32. *Many of the most unique and least redeployable intangible assets are omitted from firm balance sheets because their measurements would fail the cost-benefit test.*

PERFORMANCE EVALUATION AND
INCENTIVE PLANS

Acceptance of the wealth creation objective specifies the meaning of firm/management performance (creation of wealth) and the object of performance measurement: firm wealth. Success in most endeavors is enhanced by evaluation of one's past performance and that of parties on whom one depends, e.g., one's agents. Unfortunately, as Alchian and Demsetz (1972, p. 779) have noted, the efforts of individual members of a team do not yield readily measurable marginal products. This type of measurement error problem was discussed above under Externalities. The difficulties in measuring the contributions of individuals are, however, mitigated when the focus is on a group of people under the leadership of one management and when the activity in which they are working is to some extent separable from others. The importance of a basis for comparison (budgets, standards, other economic units, other times) is widely recognized and needs no elaboration.

Assessments of performance, typically partly based on measurements, is an inevitable accompaniment of employment and principal/agent relationships. Provisions of incentives to strengthen employees' motivations to perform well in the interests of employers is an accepted practice. In Williamson's terminology (1985, pp. 132-155), incentives may range from high-powered, in which the individual receives all of the marginal value products of his/her actions, to low-powered, in which the individual receives none of those benefits. The values, if not the risks, of medium-powered incentives, such as bonus plans, are widely recognized. "Goal congruence" is a term used to describe the alignment of an individual's interests with the firm's interests. Performance assessment, goal congruence, and incentives are bound together in the management of the firm. Accounting's role in this melange is to measure performance-relevant attributes of an activity's operations. One might expect that accounting would develop techniques for making such measurements in successful firms.

Performance reporting practices are developed under the influence of the environment. One consideration that has been emphasized by Elliot Jaques (1966, p. 17) is the concept of time span. The broader the responsibilities of an individual in an organization, the longer the period needed to evaluate his/her work. Thus, if a new recruit claims to be a journeyman machinist, the foreman can begin to form judgments about that recruit's work in a matter of hours, whereas years may pass before the decisions made by a board chairperson begin to impact earnings. It follows that performance will be reported upon more frequently at lower levels of the hierarchy.

Measurement of activity and management performance would seem to require measurement of positive and negative increments in firm wealth. "Profit center" accounting has been developed in that direction. In "cost center" accounting, management acknowledges its inability to measure revenues. In both, costs are only crudely measured. For example, typical "allocations" of costs, presumably justifiable only if they are measures of the costs of resources consumed, often are not designed and described accordingly, so are much maligned. Cost accounting is also criticized for reliance on old measurements of resource values and for omitting cost of capital. Explanations of such practices in internal reporting have eluded exogenous observers; among the hypotheses are the influence of external financial reporting and tax law (on the training and mind-set of accountants and managers) (Johnson and Kaplan, 1987, pp. 195-204), inertia, and the cost of accounting. Additional hypotheses are suggseted in Chapter 7.

33.   *Firm accounting practices have been designed to contribute to performance evaluation by measuring managers' and activities' effectiveness in contributing to the firm's wealth creation objective.*

34. *Because performance evaluation is facilitated by reference to a standard of performance, budgeting, standard costing, and comparative performance reports are commonly used in firms.*

35. *Use in performance evaluation has made comparability a prized quality of financial information: comparability over time (consistency), comparability across firms, and comparability across activities within firms.*

36. *Managers' desires to evaluate and motivate their subordinates have led to development of "responsibility accounting", which is designed to include on a subordinate's performance report all of those costs subject to the individual's control and only those costs under his/her control.*

37. *The concept of time span suggests that performance reports will be prepared more frequently for lower levels in the management hierarchy than for higher levels.*

38. *When, under the most economical operating plan, one or more major activity inputs are "fixed" in the "short run", and others vary with activity volume, short-term performance expectations might be formed accordingly, e.g., flexible budgets might be used when the prerequisite -- measurability of activity volume -- is met.*

39. *Performance measurement and reporting within firms appears to be inhibited by the influence of external reporting and tax reporting requirements, but has changed more in recent decades -- especially in firms with a multidivisional form of organization -- than has resource and product costing.*

NOTE

1. One reason not to make such an attribution is the appearance of the idea in accounting literature much earlier. See Robert Hamilton (1777/9, p. 249) as quoted by M. J. Mepham (1988, p. 67).

CHAPTER 4
THE ROLE OF CONFLICTS OF INTERESTS

Everyone thinks chiefly of his own, hardly ever of the public interest.

Attributed to Aristotle

The role of accounting in reporting on *stewardship* is a long-standing theme in accounting literature. A steward is one who is entrusted with property and responsibilities by a "master" who chooses to delegate authority to the steward. That type of relationship exists in business enterprises with absentee owners, in governmental units, and in membership organizations in addition to the original European environment where lords with large estates employed stewards. A steward's responsibility to account to his/her master in a financial report has been intimately related to the development of accounting.

A typical stewardship responsibility involved elements of bailment, employment, and possibly agency. A more recently popular research specialty in firm economics which has attracted the interest of many academic accountants is *principal-agent* relationships. Formal analyses of the conflict between the interests of a principal and those of an agent have been undertaken in that research (Baiman, 1989). Most of those researchers appear to extend the principal/agent terminology to employment and hierarchical relationships that do not involve agency in the customary legal meaning.

Firms are observed to make many *contracts* with resource suppliers and customers, so a firm could be characterized, for the purpose of this immediate discussion, as a "nexus of contracts." (Jensen and Meckling, 1976) Contracting parties always have conflicts of interests; each is seeking the best deal for himself/herself. A few firm contracts also depend on accounting numbers, thus giving persons with conflicting interests reasons to be interested in the firm's accounting. (Butterworth, Gibbins, and King, 1982)

The view taken here is that stewardship, agency and contracting are concepts that emphasize limited subsets of the total set of interest conflicts that have influenced the development of accounting in firms. The total set should be examined. Another class of interest conflicts -- those addressed in "social theory" and the literature of "critical accounting" -- are not treated as conflicts shaping the development of accounting. Thus, "worker-management" strife and poor-rich "class warfare" have not been linked to specific accounting developments, so are not discussed here.

Conflicts of interests as an influence on accounting are related to two influences discussed above. One is externalities. Conflicts of interests impair economic efficiency by causing decision makers incompletely to weigh the social costs and benefits of alternative courses of action, instead concentrating on self interests. The common results may be called Pareto suboptima or "decision externalities," or individual externalities, because certain costs or benefits are omitted from the cost/benefit analyses of decision-making individuals or groups.

The other previously-discussed influence supporting the role of conflicts of interests in the development of accounting is self-interest and opportunistic behavior. Two observations on the ubiquity of self-interest bear repeating. "(I)n all societies the typical individual continually pursues ... the increase of that (which) he can claim as his." Georgescu-Roegen, 1971, p. 320) A similar view: "The first theorem [of economics] says that individuals act so as to further their own interest, even when acting as members of a group." (Alchian, 1958, p. 352) To some, the relationship of this view to the role of the instinct for self-preservation in human evolution (or that of other species) may be of great interest, but it need not be discussed here. A point that should be made here, however, is that the generality of the self-interest tendency is not vitiated by recognition of exceptional cases in which individuals choose cooperative or even altruistic strategies that appear to be against their own interests in the short run. Also, degrees of selfishness vary across individuals and in the same individual across circumstances and times. Nevertheless, if people act somewhat selfishly on at least a substantial minority of occasions, organization structures and accounting systems must be designed to cope with that tendency. As long as, and to the extent that, individuals look out for their own interests, those interests often will conflict. Accounting has developed in an environment in which the potential for such conflicts was widely recognized and, therefore, was influential.

The theme of this chapter is that the prevalence of conflicts of interests has influenced the development of accounting in firms over several centuries. Mere mention of such familiar accounting concepts as the accountability/control approach to accounting objectives; reliability, including verifiability, neutrality, and objectivity, as a qualitative characteristic of useful financial information; and internal control, brings to mind a number of such influences. The specific nature of those influences is to be explicated in subsequent sections.

OPPORTUNISTIC BEHAVIOR

To understand the influence that conflicts of interests have had on the development of accounting in firms, one should consider the extent to which firm constituents have been aware of the potential effects of such conflicts -- influence presumably is associated with awareness -- over the long period during which accounting developed to its present state. Without embarking on a major historical project, a sampling of the views of several astute observers can give one some idea of eighteenth, nineteenth, and twentieth century thinking. Thus, Adam Smith is unlikely to have been the only late eighteenth-century observer to have noted that directors, being managers of other people's money rather than their own, could not be expected to "watch over it with the same anxious vigilance with which the partners in a copartnery frequently watch over their own." (1776/1976, p. 741) Later, John Stuart Mill echoed Smith's view:

> "But experience shows, and proverbs, the expression of popular experience, attest, how inferior is the quality of hired servants, compared with the ministration of those personally interested in the work, and how indispensable, when hired service must be employed, is 'the master's eye' to watch over it." (1849/1965, p. 137)

At the turn of the twentieth century, Alfred Marshall (1895) warned that absentee owners must guard against managers taking kickbacks, shirking, and engaging in nepotism (p. 383) and addressed the issue of monitoring costs in large organizations (p. 365). Note that all three of these authors were concerned with the conflict between owners and hired managers, perhaps because that particular conflict was relatively new, having been brought to the fore by the spread of joint stock companies in England in the eighteenth and nineteenth centuries. One might assume that conflicts between an owner and his employees, suppliers, and customers were so generally understood as not to warrant comment.

A current commentator on the behavior of people in firms suggests: "A healthy regard for opportunism is essential to an understanding of the purposes served by complex modes of economic organization," (Williamson, 1985, p. 388) presumably including the accounting and control systems of those complex organizations. He defined opportunism as "self-interest seeking with guile" (p. 47), including, in the language of risk analysis, both adverse selection (ex ante) and moral hazard (ex post). Further examples of opportunistic behavior in firms are outright theft, fraud, shirking and free riding, acceptance of unintended perquisites, nepotism, empire building, and use of company funds to further one's personal position in, or outside of, the firm. Management (manipulation?) of reported earnings is another area, as exemplified by Healy's conclusion: "Bonus schemes create incentives for managers to select accounting procedures and accruals to maximize the value of their bonus awards." (1985, p. 106) Deliberate falsification of reports is included below in connection with self-biased views.

Owner-Manager Conflicts

One type of conflict of interests that leads to some of the more subtle types of opportunistic behavior is that between absentee owners and managers of a firm. The interests of property owners are quite clear and have always been so: rights to the economic benefits that the property yields and the ultimate power over it. The interests of managers are not so clear. One might consider three: (1) personal gain, which may be subdivided into pecuniary and psychological streams; (2) feelings associated with duty, loyalty, devotion, and obligation to the employing owners; and (3) altruistic motivations. Recognition that different managers might give different weights to those three interests suggests that interested observers might also differ in their views. The question is further complicated by consideration of varying horizons: the second interest mentioned above, which might be abbreviated to "duty," is easily interpreted as a long-run approach to personal gain. With regard to altruism, students of business may be reluctant to claim expertise in assessing the weight to be accorded to corporate managers' altruistic feelings towards owners and other constituents. Is it safe to bet that most managers are motivated primarily by the desire for personal gain? Let's proceed on that assumption.

The conflict of interests under discussion was explained clearly by Berle and Means (1932, p. 122).

> If we are to assume that the desire for *personal profit* is the prime force motivating control, we must conclude that the interests of control are different from and often radically opposed to those of ownership;   that the owners most emphatically will not be served by a profit-seeking controlling group. In the operation of the corporation, the controlling group, even if they own a large block of stock, can serve their own pockets better by profiting at the expense of the company than by making profits for it. If such persons can make a profit of a million dollars from a sale of property to the corporation, they can afford to suffer a loss of $600,000 through the ownership of 60 per cent of the stock, since the transaction will still net them $400,000 and the remaining stockholders will shoulder the corresponding loss. As their proportion of the holdings decrease, and both profits and losses of the company accrue less and less to them, the opportunities of profiting at the expense of the corporation accrue more directly to their benefit. When their holdings amount to only such fractional per cents as the holdings of the management in management-controlled corporations, profits at the expense of the corporation become practically clear gain to the persons in control and the interests of a profit-seeking control run directly counter to the interests of the owners.

Shareholder-Creditor Conflicts

A quite different type of conflict of interests that presents the potential for opportunistic behavior also occurs in the corporate form of organization, viz., the conflict between creditors and shareholders. In this context, the essence of the corporation is a deal between shareholders and creditors that is enforced by the chartering body, a state in the case of the typical American corporation, the federal government in other American cases, and other sovereign governments in other countries. Shareholders undertake to maintain stated capital as a buffer for the protection of creditors in exchange for a limitation on their liability for corporate debts to the amounts invested. Corporate creditors grant the shareholders protection of their personal assets from corporate creditors' claims (limited liability) in consideration of shareholders agreeing to maintain corporate stated capital.

The type of opportunistic behavior that this "corporate deal" is designed to protect creditors against is the firm making an investment having a distribution of probable outcomes with the lower tail in the negative range. (See Smith and Warner, 1979, p. 117.) Stated capital is intended to absorb such negative payoffs, so they will not be borne by creditors. A major example of failure of that arrangement due to the subversion of creditors' interest in debtors' financial soundness occurred in a number of American savings and loan associations in the 1980's. The traditional caution of lenders (depositors in this case) was subverted by the government's deposit insurance, thus allowing risk-taking managements to attract vast deposits into failing "banks." The other ways that conflicts of interests, including those involving accountants and auditors contributed to savings and loan associations' difficulties will not be described here.

The "corporate deal" has influenced the development of accounting by putting more emphasis on the distinction between capital (to be maintained) and income (available for dividends)

than was recognized in unincorporated firms. But one must
take care not to attribute emphasis on the distinction between
capital and income entirely to the corporate form. The
increasing importance of large aggregations of fixed assets in
firms leading the mercantile and industrial "revolutions" of the
eighteenth and nineteenth centuries no doubt contributed to
concern with the distinction between expenditures to be
capitalized and those to be expensed and with depreciation
accounting and other deferrals and accruals, even in
partnerships and sole proprietorships.

Empire Building

   "Empire building" was mentioned above as a type of
potential opportunistic behavior by people in organizations.
Students of organizations recognize that managers commonly
feel more important when they have responsibility for more
assets and have more people working under their direction.
Furthermore, evidence has been reported that managers'
compensation is directly associated with the number of
subordinates and number of layers in the hierarchy beneath
them. (Leonard, 1990) Therefore, managers' self-interest favors
increasing the size of the organization or part of organization
that they manage. Also, as Chandler pointed out (1977, p. 10)
in his explanation of the increasing role of "the visible hand" of
management in modern, multiunit enterprises, "For salaried
managers, the continuing existence of their enterprises was
essential to their lifetime careers." Consequently, " ... in
making administrative decisions, career managers preferred
policies that favored the long-term stability and growth of their
enterprises to those that maximized current profits."
Augmentation of owners' wealth, on the other hand, is
associated with return on the firm's investments, residual
income (net present value), increasing earnings per share, and
share price. Accordingly, one might expect that management-
controlled firms tend to emphasize growth of revenues, assets,

and aggregate earnings, while owner-managed firms tend to stress return on investment, residual income, earnings per share, and share price. The relationship between managers' bonus contracts and their choices of accounting policies was mentioned above.

Influences on the Development of Accounting

The general point made in the preceding paragraphs is that the phenomenon of opportunistic behavior by firm constituents is not a twentieth-century discovery by one individual but was generally recognized by owners, managers, lenders, and lawmakers over a long period of accounting history. The effects that such general recognition has had on the development of accounting and control procedures in firms are familiar to people with substantial experience in organizations. Unfortunately, the importance of guarding against opportunistic behavior when designing, operating and depending upon financial reporting systems is so seldom explicitly emphasized that practitioners and teachers may forget it and students may fail to gain a full appreciation of it until bitter experience makes a firm impression.

In general, awareness of the risks of opportunistic behavior has led to development of techniques for controlling, counteracting, or channelling opportunistic tendencies so as to achieve the objectives of those in charge. On the relatively positive side, one sees behavior-motivating devices such as standards and budgets, performance reporting in general and "responsibility accounting" in particular, and incentive compensation schemes. Techniques with more negative implications include internal control devices such as auditing, bonding, double-entry accounting systems, and a variety of "internal check" techniques including physical safeguards, separation of powers, and document controls. If one could imagine an organization whose personnel were limited to absolutely loyal members of one large family, one might visualize the possibilities for eliminating many of the control devices that are common in typical firms. Of course, controls aimed at prevention and detection of honest errors and protection of assets from outsiders would still be needed.

Another important accounting development to which the conflict of interests between owners and management -- or the stewardship responsibility -- is believed to have contributed is periodic reporting. In both partnerships and joint stock companies it became common for some of the owners not to be involved in the day-to-day management of the firm. Reporting to "absentee owners" on a periodic basis appears to have become common practice, for obvious reasons. In earlier times, sole proprietorships, family businesses, and working partnerships presumably were the pattern, along with the occasional single-purpose venture. Periodic closings of books were not the normal practice in those circumstances.

This section can be summarized in a series of four propositions regarding the effects of opportunistic behavior on the development of accounting in firms:

40.   *Widespread use of the corporate form of organization, in which the interests of creditors and owners are explicitly recognized as conflicting so that dividends are limited to the amounts of earnings, resulted in greater emphasis on the distinction between capital and income than otherwise would have been the case.*

41.   *Because the interests of firm managers are furthered by increase in firm size, and the interests of owners are furthered by firm profitability, one might predict that firms with relatively unconcentrated ownership, or with directors owning a small percentage of the shares, emphasize growth of revenues, assets and aggregate earnings, whereas "owner-managed" firms emphasize levels of return on investment, residual income, earnings per share, and share price.*

42. *Absentee ownership in large partnerships and joint stock companies contributed to the development of periodic financial reporting.*

43. *The prevalence of opportunistic and self-interested behavior leads to incorporation of control features such as double entry, bonding, auditing, physical safeguards, separation of powers, and document controls.*

SELF-BIASED VIEWS IN FINANCIAL REPORTING

Here we are concerned with the general desire of individuals to make a favorable impression on others. Two bases for this desire may be identified: (1) ego, and (2) self interest. They often work together to bias one's oral or written report on his/her own behavior in a favorable direction. For example, we seldom hear reports of arguments in which the reporter was wrong, or of a student who feels he/she was given too high a mark. Related to the tendency to view one's personal performance favorably is the tendency to have a high opinion of organizations to which one belongs: loyalty. People tend to form a biased view of the qualities possessed by the department, division, firm, school, political subdivision, or nation to which they "belong." In this section, the influence that recognition of the tendency to self-biased views has had on the development of accounting and auditing is outlined.

The parallel between company financial reports and students' grade reports -- both of which report on performance -- is widely recognized. Managers hate to get a poor grade (mark), especially a failing grade (loss), or a worse grade than they got last term (decline in earnings). One is bound to recognize that managers have a great deal of control over the numbers that are reported in financial statements -- often less control than they would like to have but more control than those relying on the statements would prefer. The frequency and degree of influence exerted due to the stimulus of self-bias clearly is not measurable. Like other forms of opportunistic behavior, it typically is not a permanent, explicit pattern but is resorted to only in "emergencies." "I don't plan to make this fiddling a habit." Nevertheless, to the user of financial reports, the influence of such manipulation on the information conveyed must be judged very substantial.

In addition to emergency circumstances, another excuse for such manipulation is that the same bending of the numbers that is in management's interest is in the interest of reportees.

> ... [E]ven if accounting concepts were absolutely clear and there were no difficulties in valuation, there would still remain the fact that directors who are responsible for signing the balance sheet may feel quite genuinely that it is in the best interest of the company to under-estimate profits in one year and to over-estimate them in another, while the auditors acting in all sincerity accept the view of the directors. That is to say, the position under the Companies Act, 1929 and the general tenor of case law decisions seems to be that inaccuracy and a deliberate intention to mislead may be condoned in certain circumstances. In view of the fact that the [user] never knows in the case of an individual company how far these circumstances are operating he cannot with absolute confidence use the balance sheet figures. (Coase, Edwards and Fowler, 1938, p. 3)

In more modern jargon, smoothing of earnings is desirable to reduce the apparent risk in a company's securities and its cost of capital. Finding ways to avoid reporting a decline in earnings is good for the stock price and for the shareholders.

The impact of reporters' self-bias on the numbers in financial reports can take the form of "liberal" reporting or of "smoothing." In this context, liberal reporting means attempting to convey a more favorable impression than alternative reporting would convey. Thus, the choice of classifying an asset or liability as current or noncurrent affects the "current ratio" and net working capital. The choice of treating a contract as off balance sheet or recognizing it on the balance sheet affects the debt-equity ratio. On the income statement, the liberally inclined reporter prefers that debits be classified as extraordinary charges, discontinuances, or accounting changes, but that credits be placed in the continuing operations section. Most importantly, the liberal reporter prefers choices that give higher current earnings and owners' equity.

Smoothing

Except for the (presumably rare) case of the long-run, deliberate manipulator, the dominant form of self-bias in financial reporting is smoothing of earnings. There can be little doubt but that, among managers, the ideal pattern of earnings is one of steady growth. When the economic environment combines with management performance to yield departures from that ideal pattern, management naturally seeks to use accounting choices to report earnings as close to the ideal as possible. According to this interpretation, a period's results, prior to accounting manipulation, tend to fall into one of four categories:

1. So good that something should be held back in the form of secret reserves for a "rainy day" (see 3 below).
2. On target, so normal reporting is appropriate.
3. Below target so as to threaten the image: secret reserves should be called on to obscure the shortfall.
4. Obviously terrible: take a "big bath" including the creation of secret reserves for future use.

Thus, smoothing typically involves both conservative accounting, when times are good, and liberal accounting, when times are bad.

To the extent that this attitude, which is difficult to prove but is almost universally believed to prevail among managers "except in our company," is subconsciously accepted, it is bound to lead to some degree of deception of reportees. It tends to obscure the effects of risky policies. The strength of managers' feelings on this subject was reflected in violent opposition to the FASB's Statement No. 5, which requires that firms choosing to bear insurable risks, rather than insuring against them, report the results as they occur. Managements' positions on a long string of other standards-setting issues (SFAS Nos. 12, 15, 25, 52, 87, 89) support the hypothesis that managers have (often successfully) sought (1) to retain control over calculations of earnings, and (2) to win acceptance of methods that tend to smooth reported earnings, at the cost of deceiving external users of financial reports. (Armstrong, 1977; Kelly-Newton, 1980, p. 44; Staubus, 1985)

Managers' interests in smoothing earnings have been recognized and understood over a period long enough to influence the development of accounting standards, as the above 1938 reference indicates. Further support comes from the distinguished economist, Sir Josiah Stamp.

> There is a fairly general practice of minimizing results in good years and maximizing them in bad years through stock, debt and security valuations and other secret reserves (and releases from reserves ...) (1932, p. 660)

For a remarkable current story illlustrating a wide variety of smoothing techniques used in one company, see "Managing Profits: How General Electric Damps Fluctuations in its Annual Earnings." (*Wall Street Journal*, 1994)

In recent years, a number of researchers have sought empirical evidence of smoothing of earnings. (A recent example is Stinson (1991).) For a review of much of that research, see Schipper (1989). In general, the results indicate that quantitative empirical research methods are ill suited to the task, although the potentially spectacular results have tempted several to embark on such a research exercise. In the eyes of experienced practitioners, such exercises give empirical research in accounting a bad name.

Conservatism

The motivations for conservative financial reporting are complex and extend beyond self-bias by reporters. Perhaps conservatism is an innate human tendency that is not always offset by the bias towards reporting one's own performance in a favorable light. When the latter bias wins out, managers presumably embrace conservative reporting only to permit smoothing of earnings. If so, it must be limited to "good times" when reported earnings need not be maximized, or to acceptance of an apparently conservative accounting policy that offers more in stability than it costs in level of earnings. Thus, adherence to "historical cost" in an era of generally rising but fluctuating nominal prices prevents managers' exposure to the tyranny of volatile current market prices while, typically, building up a reservoir of both instant earnings and instant losses that can be fed into income to achieve the desired earnings pattern. If a conservative bias not directed towards smoothing of earnings is common, perhaps it is manifested in classification choices that do not affect net income. Is there any evidence on that hypothesis?

Looking beyond managers, a preference for conservative financial reporting may be associated with the observation that unfavorable surprises have greater negative consequences than favorable surprises have positive consequences. In more technical terms, an "asymmetric loss function" might lead auditors, preparers, and users of financial reports to prefer downside estimating errors to upside errors. That preference could extend beyond estimating errors to include outright conservative misstatements of line items to offset possible overestimates of the income effects of other line items.

Another hypothesis is that those who save and invest are inclined to "hold something back for a rainy day" in real economic terms, so may also be inclined to the same tendency in financial reports. Investors and lenders who use financial statements may have such a strong conservative financial reporting bias that preparers attempt to accommodate it. Those managers with a fiduciary responsibility, such as bankers and trustees of nonbusiness organizations, may be similarly inclined. When all of these motivations, and others, are considered, a conclusion that conservatism in financial reporting is due to conflicts of interests is not warranted.

The general tendency towards self-bias in financial reporting has led to a specific measurement bias: managements rarely deflate financial data pertaining to different dates to eliminate the effects of changes in the monetary measuring unit. Managers oppose inflation accounting because (1) it generally reduces the nominal amount of reported earnings; (2) it wipes out most reservoirs of instant earnings (undervalued assets), thus reducing managers' flexibility in reporting a steady uptrend in earnings; and (3) it eliminates much of the nominal growth of earnings and other measures of size. All three of these points fit the hypothesis that because managers are biased towards favorable reporting of their own performance, they oppose "inflation accounting."

Effects on Reporters' Utility

Another approach to understanding reporters' interest in manipulating financial statements is through the analysis of net benefits. Manipulation is not seen as a zero-sum game, despite its zero effect on a firm's lifetime earnings. For one thing, lifetime earnings are not an important concept to a manager with a short tenure in office. For example, if a newly appointed manager can take a "big bath" that is blamed on his/her predecessor while building a reservoir of future earnings through excessive write-downs, he/she sees a gain. Secondly, there is a net gain in utility from taking a dollar of earnings from a peak for filling a trough, given a concave utility function. Third, manipulation through classification within the balance sheet or within the income statement is not offset in another period. Finally, the strength of a manager's time preference when he/she is convinced he/she is a victim of temporary circumstances, so only needs to stretch the truth this one time, should not be underestimated.

Empire building was discussed above. Now that smoothing of earnings and the growth cult have been recognized, a popular route to all three management goals can be mentioned. Diversification -- not inaptly called "deworseification" by Peter Lynch (1989, p. 146) -- can, if successful, produce earnings stability (through the portfolio effect), earnings growth, and general growth of management's empire that justifies higher compensation -- an almost irresistible combination available to the nonowner manager.

The above discussion leads to three hypotheses regarding the impact of managers' self-bias on financial reporting:

44. *Managers can be expected to lean towards financial reporting choices that make themselves look better, so often will choose (1) the more "liberal" alternative measurement or classification and (2) income-smoothing techniques.*

45. *The widespread practice of reporting certain classes of assets at their historical cost (and liabilities at their historical proceeds) is explained, in part, by the preferences of those managers who hope to call on reserves of instant earnings and instant losses to build a record of steady growth in reported earnings.*

46. *Because managers are biased towards favorable reporting of their own performance, they prefer "nominal dollar accounting," that is, failure to deflate financial data pertaining to different measurement*

dates, especially comparative income statements, for changes in the monetary measuring unit.

Reportees' Understanding and Response

If we understand the ways in which managements' self-biased behavior is reflected in financial reports, we should also understand that readers of those reports cannot be expected to ignore such behavior -- given time to catch on to it. If other parties interested in financial reporting have not responded, the system is out of equilibrium. Indeed, even preparers have recognized that curbing the more flagrant abuses is in their interests. Consequently, a number of aspects of financial reporting have been developed in response to the recognition that the interests of managers/preparers/reporters conflict with those of the public/users/reportees. Starting with the more specific technical features of generally accepted accounting principles, then moving to more general and institutional features, the following propositions seem easy to support:

47. *Managers' preferences for taking credit for all good things that happen in a business while making excuses for unfavorable occurrences has led to rules minimizing and controlling classification of various "non-recurring events" such as prior period adjustments, extraordinary items, unusual or infrequent items, discontinued operations, accounting changes, and quasi-reorganizations. Except for items meeting specified criteria, the all-inclusive view of income is reflected in GAAP, contrary to the natural preferences of managers.*

48. *To counter managements' liberal bias, auditors and users (especially bankers) have encouraged development of conservative practices, such as the lower-of-cost-and-market rule for current assets, the "realization principle" for recognizing revenue, and the treatment of many costs as period expenses instead of*

adding them to asset accounts for future matching with the resulting revenues. Broad examples of the latter are a variety of asset holding costs (most interest, property taxes, insurance, storage costs) and intangible investments such as research and development, human resources development, and start-up costs.[1]

49. *In recognition of preparers' self-interest in financial reporting, the broad qualitative standard labelled "reliability" in Statement of Financial Accounting Concepts No. 2 (FASB, 1980), including verifiability and neutrality, is valued by those who recognize conflicts of interests among constituent groups.*

50. *Consistency in the application of accounting principles over time has become generally accepted in response to managements' abuse of their right to change accounting principles to permit them to reflect the picture they would like readers to see.[2]*

51. *The practice of employing an "external auditor" to pass judgment on a company's financial reporting has developed to curb management's expressions of self-bias in the reports.*

52. *Regulatory mechanisms have been established to assist the parties with interests in financial reporting in developing reporting standards that are not entirely controlled by managements, as they might otherwise be.*

CONCLUDING COMMENTS

The prevalence of conflicts of interests among firm constituents has been a major influence shaping the development of accounting in firms. The view here is that insufficient attention has been paid in accounting literature, especially textbooks, to the importance of those conflicts. The necessity to guard against opportunistic behavior and self-bias when designing, operating, and depending on financial reporting systems is so rarely explicitly explained that students (and others) may fail to gain a full appreciation of it. More emphasis needs to be put on the natural tendency of managers to be deeply concerned about how their performance is reported and on the potential for different parties to have different objectives for financial reporting: to inform, or to convey the image they would like others to see (which might involve disinformation) in order to meet strategic goals. The natural basis for the development of financial reporting practices that serve the interests of reporters, rather than reportees, should be understood. He who controls the information system should be expected to use it to his own advantage. It is fanciful to expect objectivity.

A healthy regard for the impacts that interest conflicts can have on behavior might lead one to suspect various influences on the development of accounting and auditing beyond those proposed above. The seven propositions that follow may be viewed as hypotheses for further thought and research.

53. *Management's special interest in financial reporting practices has led them to prize certain qualities in those practices and the results from applying them: stability (smoothing) of reported earnings, flexibility and management control of income reporting, and conservatism when it results in building "hidden reserves" that can be called on to smooth reported earnings. (See Staubus, 1985)*

54. *Management's substantial degree of control over the selection of financial reporting methods in the past, and their continuing heavy influence on the standards-setting process has resulted in the above-mentioned qualities being built into GAAP. One should not expect managements' voluntary acquiescence in any major change in external reporting standards that impairs those qualities.[3]*

55. *When the evaluatee controls the performance evaluation techniques and process, evaluations have less credibility than when they are based on an independent process. Therefore, firm financial reports are not valued as highly by external parties as they might be if financial reporting were not substantially controlled by management.*

56. *In-firm accountants whose future success and rewards are heavily dependent on the perceived success of their firm or firm segment and on evaluations by their management superiors are easily persuaded that top management's view of its own performance is accurate.*

57. *External auditors are more closely associated with auditees (managers) than with (external) reportees (users). Internal auditors are more closely associated with their reportees (top managers) than with their auditees (lower level managers). This leads to the prediction that internal auditors will report more critically than will external auditors.*

58. *External auditors' closer association with management than with shareholders often results in their acceptance of management's view of events rather than an independent, objective view of those events, thus reducing the value of financial reports to reportees.*

59. *Auditors are torn by conflicting motivations: (1) recognition of the need, in many cases, to counter management's bias towards liberal reporting with their own conservatism, (2) a tendency towards friendly agreement with the management personnel that engage them and with whom they socialize (much more than with shareholders), and (3) the risk of incurring liability to those relying on auditors' reports, especially in recent decades (in certain countries). Those conflicts weigh differently on different auditors and at different times, thus leading to a demand for regulation of auditing.*

NOTES

1. R. J. Ball (1989, p. 41) offers another explanation for acceptance of the lower-of-cost-and-market valuation rule. Verification of departures from cost is costly, so auditors only accept those that run counter to management's interests, i.e., in a conservative direction. Auditors presume that such departures are correct; in any event, little harm is done if they are not.

2. A more cynical explanation for the consistency requirement credits its acceptance to the preferences of managements: it clearly impedes changes in reporting principles -- exactly what management (who developed the present principles) want.

3. It seems clear that managers prize their power over the standards setting process and seek to maintain that power. For example, they prefer the more pliable private sector standards setting body over a less easily influenced public sector body. In the American case, one might speculate regarding the percentage of influence on the Financial Accounting Standards Board wielded by "management." Eighty percent? Ninety percent? What other group that is not influenced by management exerts significant pressure on standards setters?

    One explanation of the imbalance of power applied in the standards-setting process is that managers have more at stake than the typical shareholder or creditor: a relatively larger portion of the manager's personal wealth plus his/her ego.

CHAPTER 5
SIZE OF FIRM

Three evolving characteristics of a firm provide major features of the environment in which accounting develops: its size, its expansion strategy, and its organizational structure. They appear as Tier III influences in EXHIBIT I on page 149. The proposition that the immense size of a few nineteenth century firms and many twentieth century firms is intertwined with developments in accounting may go unopposed. But the specific influences of size on accounting have not been addressed systematically. A review of the economics literature on size, or scale, provide a good base for thinking about the influence of large size on firm accounting. Similarly, an attempt is made to understand firms' movements towards vertical integration and horizontal diversification in an effort to find links with accounting. Finally, the relationships between accounting and the two pure forms of business organization -- the functional, or unitary, form and the product division form -- are examined.

Issues relating to the size of firm long have interested economists, but perhaps not as long as some other matters. Size in itself was given little attention by the early English classicists. Adam Smith (1776), David Ricardo (1821), and James Mill (1821) were fascinated by the efficiency advantages of the specialization (division) of labor, but did not pay much attention to other economies of scale. John Stuart Mill, on the other hand, included a chapter in his *Principles* (1848, Chapter ix, Book I) entitled "Of Production on a Large, and Production on a Small Scale." That chapter actually concentrated on the advantages of large scale production; the only limiting factor Mill mentioned was the size of the market. Farming was the only field for which the merits of both large and small scale were addressed, and no generally applicable principles came out of that discussion (pp. 142-152).

Textbooks in the neoclassical tradition (for example, Marshall, 1895, Book IV, Chapters viii to xiii) and Stigler (1947, Chapters 7, 8) and modern books (Thompson, 1981, Chapters 7, 8) have routinely analyzed economies and diseconomies of scale. But those analyses differ. Marshall and Stigler concentrated on scale of plant; Thompson deals explicitly with scale of firm separately from scale of plant.

In the present work, the effects on accounting of indivisibilities and economies of scale in acquisitions have already been discussed (in Chapter 2). Specialization of labor also affects accounting to the extent that it may create an interest in cost data on separate activities at the same time that it makes the gathering of such data easier by assigning workers to separate tasks on a full-time basis.   Most importantly, economies of accounting scale have been developed in large firms; the mere mention of data processing hardware and software suggests the vast changes in the basic systems of accounting that would not have occurred if all firms, and other organizations, had remained small. The primary concerns of this chapter, however, are with economies and diseconomies of firm scale with special attention to the diseconomies stemming from coordination problems, control loss, incentive erosion, and bureaucracy.

ECONOMIES OF FIRM SCALE

Three areas of economies of *firm* scale have been identified. One is the same specialization-of-work factor that operates at the *plant* level; large firms can divide the headquarters work among more specialists. Considering the differences between plant work and headquarters work, specialization may be even more helpful at the latter level: "The greatest economies arising from the division of labor ... are those that accrue to economizing on attention and cognition as scarce resources." (Masten, 1986, p. 447) Secondly,

> Quite apart from any effect an increase in scale may have on production costs is the increasing monopoly power often associated with greater size. As a firm grows larger its ability to influence the prices, price policies, and general behavior of its competitors in a manner favorable to itself increases. This may take various forms, but in general the change is reflected in the demand curve for the product the firm sells and not in the cost curves. (Buchanan, 1940, p. 306)

The ability of large firms to influence others to their own advantage is not limited to competitors. Suppliers may offer lower prices or better service either on the basis of real cost savings or for other reasons. Customers and financial institutions may see advantages to dealing with large firms. Also, a perhaps increasingly important factor is the power of large firms in government relations, including lobbying and influence on elections.

A third factor contributing to returns to scale of firm is information (Arrow, 1988). Because a bit of information is indivisible, a small firm cannot buy a fraction of a bit related to its size. To have as good an information set as a large firm, the small firm must spend approximately the same absolute amount, i.e., a larger percentage of its revenues. Thus, large firms can have better information for the same cost (relative to revenues) as a small firm, so can earn superior returns.[1] Market research and production technology research are good examples. One is tempted to speculate that accounting information fits this pattern too, but no example of an indivisible bit of accounting information providing a larger payoff in a large firm than in a small one, but with equal costs, comes to mind. Ordinary economies of scale may be enjoyed by large accounting operations, of course, including savings from use of large scale equipment.

DISECONOMIES OF FIRM SCALE

The factors contributing to increasing returns to size present an impressive case for the efficiency of large plants and large firms. Indeed, one "might therefore expect to see large firms driving their smaller rivals completely out of many branches of industry, yet they do not in fact do so." (Marshall, 1895, p. 371) Later (1933, pp. 10-12) P. Sargant Florence could see no upper bound on the most efficient scale of production. When the advantages of vertical integration and diversification are added to those of large scale, one might wonder: "Why is not all production carried on by one big firm?" (Coase, 1937, p. 394) This line of thought leads to a search for diseconomies of firm scale. Without using that term, Marshall, in a passage worth repeating, led the way:

> On the other hand the small employer has advantages of his own. The master's eye is everywhere; there is no shirking by his foremen or workmen, no divided responsibility, no sending half-understood messages backwards and forwards from one department to another. He saves much of the book-keeping, and nearly all of the cumbrous system of checks that are necessary in the business of a large firm ....
> (1895, p. 365)

Marshall, it is fair to say, understood the management inefficiencies characterizing large organizations, but it remained for E.A.G. Robinson to specify coordination as the factor limiting the optimum size of a firm (1931, p. 44). Kaldor added the technical interpretation: the supply of coordinating skill is an indivisible (fixed) factor because coordination cannot be shared.

> You cannot increase the supply of co-ordinating
> ability available to an enterprise alongside an
> increase in the supply of other factors, as it is
> the essence of coordination that every single
> decision should be made on a comparison with
> all the other decisions already made or likely to
> be made; it must therefore pass through a
> single brain. (Kaldor, 1934, p. 68)

Thus, once a firm has found the optimal (lowest cost) recipe,
any attempt to increase production by adding quantities of all
inputs except one (coordination) moves the firm to a higher cost
recipe.

The Robinson/Kaldor interpretation has been widely
accepted (Stigler, 1947, p. 138; DeSerpa, 1985, p. 214)
although Edith Penrose, writing 25 years after Kaldor (1959, p.
12), argued that no one had yet established that managerial
coordination was a fixed rather than a variable input. Certainly,
one is bound to question whether coordination is the whole
story. In management, coordination generally refers to the
various functional fields and other parts of an organization
working together to achieve organizational objectives. Kaldor,
as quoted above, emphasized choosing from among alternative
courses of action, i.e., decision making. His point was that one
person (or group, such as a board) must be informed about all
those alternatives from among which he/she chooses.
Papandreou (1952, pp. 190-191) saw the delegation of much
coordination work but retention of the tasks of "peak
coordination" by an individual or a group that works as a single
agency in seeking "the internal and external equilibria of the
system ... simultaneously against the constellation of data
confronting the firm." The decision maker can delegate the
tasks of gathering and quantifying information regarding the
alternatives, and the advent of such aids as computers and
expert systems relieves him/her of significant work. But not all
relevant aspects of a course of action can be quantified, nor can
the weights given to several subjective factors be reduced to a

formula for multiple-criteria decision making. Perhaps "All changes which improve managerial technique will tend to increase the size of the firm" (Coase, 1937, p. 397), but the limited capacity of a top manager or management team may well be a critical factor in limiting that size. One interpretation is that top management service is a fixed-elastic input that can be stretched, but at some cost and at the risk of breaking, so no clear-cut optimum is discernible. None of these interpretations permits one completely to dismiss Kaldor's view of the indivisibility of coordination. Accordingly, anything accounting can contribute to coordination may raise the upper bound on firm size.

Another probable diseconomy of scale lies in the general area of losses of information and increased costs in the communication processes used in large organizations, as discussed in Chapter 2 under "information losses in transmission." Bounded rationality and opportunism are, once more, the underlying factors. Related developments in accounting were mentioned in Proposition 21.

CONTROL LOSS

Information losses in the course of intrafirm transmission lead to control loss. The introduction of this term by Williamson (1970, pp. 25-35) was accompanied by a complex model that incorporated variables such as span of control and number of hierarchical levels. As applied to large organizations, the term is self-explanatory and widely accepted. Marshall's recitation of the advantages of the "small employer," while not clearly focused on control loss, certainly alluded to it. (See page 84 above.) Downs' "Law of Diminishing Control" expresses the concept succinctly: "The larger any organization becomes, the weaker is the control over its actions exercised by those at the top." (1967, p. 143)

The concept of control loss rests firmly on two more basic factors discussed earlier: bounded rationality and opportunistic behavior. Consider the latter. Do conflicts of interest among people at various hierarchical levels contribute to control loss? Surely they do! Each interface of levels must provide modest opportunities for individuals to further their self-interest -- e.g., to build personal empires -- by (1) modifying the intentions of top management as policies are interpreted and executed and (2) biassing the information that moves up, as in the case of requests for capital expenditures. The more hierarchical levels in an organization, the greater the opportunities for control loss. That provides a firm basis for agreeing with Williamson's conclusion that "the cumulative effects of control loss are fundamentally responsible for limitations to firm size," (1970, p. 31) as Boulding suggested (1968, p. 8).

A broad set of accounting procedures that may be largely explained by management's and owners' concern about loss of control (in the context of opportunism and bounded rationality) is that set devoted to facilitating operating activities and maintenance of internal control, especially via internal check techniques. Thus, the evolution of procedures associated with cash receipts and disbursements, payroll, purchasing, and "inventory control" has kept pace with the growth of firms to limit control loss.

INCENTIVE DILUTION

Refer once more to the Marshall quote (above) regarding the advantages of the small employer: "[T]here is no shirking by his foremen or workmen." In the discussion under the heading *Externalities*, the point was made that the best cost-benefit matching occurs in one-person economic units, because that person reaps all of the benefits of his/her actions and bears all of the costs (subject to externalities). Considering a variety of sizes and forms of economic units and parts thereof, an individual may reap anywhere between zero and 100 percent of the benefits and bear anywhere between zero and 100 percent of the costs of his/her actions. (One might even imagine cases in which that range would be extended.)

Now divide the benefits and the costs into pecuniary and nonpecuniary classes, and focus on the latter. The types of nonpecuniary benefits typically enjoyed by a one-person firm, such as an artisan, do not generally reach the employee buried deep in the factory or office of a huge firm. Neither the customer's pleasure nor the beauty of the finished product are fully enjoyed by the person machining a part or transcribing data. Nor do negative responses reach the individual directly or immediately. Praise and censure from a superior may substitute in various degrees, but one might reasonably surmise that nonpecuniary costs and benefits are matched and tied to the individual less satisfactorily in large firms than in small ones. In general, managers in large organizations are handicapped in their ability to trace or associate individuals' actions and their consequences, thus providing a degree of anonymity -- the opportunist's friend -- that leads to shirking and excessive consumption of perquisites. Also, work in large firms often is said to be less fulfilling to the individual, so it is possible that large firms typically have higher employment costs for a given labor service than do small firms. In general, one might expect that techniques would be devised to respond to such problems, that those techniques might be costly, and that they might involve accounting.

BUREAUCRATIC COSTS

Bureaucratic costs appear to be another factor to be reckoned with in relation to limits on the size of firms. The negative economic aspect of bureaucracy was recognized by Marshall (1920, p. 304): "[E]xperience shows creative ideas and experiments in business technique, and in business organization, to be ... not very common in private enterprises which have drifted toward bureaucratic methods as the result of their great age and large size." In more recent decades, Tullock

(1965), Niskanen (1971), and Olson (1986) have called attention to economic aspects of bureaucracy, and Williamson (1985, pp. 148-153) has addressed specific characteristics of bureaucracy that handicap large businesses. One is the instrumental propensity to manage: "Decision-makers project a capacity to manage complexity that is repeatedly refuted by events." (p. 149) Managers tend to have confidence in their ability to cope with future problems -- perhaps excessive confidence. Another common economic weakness of bureaucracies is opportunistic behavior of individuals that is not consistent with professed organizational objectives. Empire building, position perpetuation, and bias toward the field and the people one knows can lead to logrolling for the approval of projects, retention of people who do not pull their own weight, and other inefficiencies.

> I want to stress that what gets this bureaucratic "misery" all started is the loss of performance measures higher up in the hierarchy. The integrity of subjective evaluations is a function of the monitor's incentives. An owner will not have to worry about bribes from an employee. If he accepts personal services in exchange for higher bonuses, this is merely an efficient trade. But when the monitor does not bear all the financial consequences of his actions, such trades will be excessive. (Holmstrum, 1988, p. 28)

Successful, continuing, large firms can be expected to seek means of counteracting such bureaucratic inefficiencies. A general theme of such means is likely to be detailed information in a form that tends to shed light on opportunistic bureaucratic behavior. Thus, performance reports comparing budgeted against actual costs, comparisons of function costs across operating units, either in the same firm or across firms, and finer classifications of information than otherwise might be justified can be expected in large firms.

Coordination as a fixed (indivisible) factor; control loss and related communication problems; incentive erosion due to dilution of cost and benefit incidence; and bureaucratic costs -- some combination of these, and perhaps other, factors support the "management problems" explanation for the presence of many firms instead of just one huge one. A non-management factor that may handicap large businesses is the bias against bigness that is detectable, perhaps to various degrees, in decentralized economics. For example, "Unions have had their greatest success in dealing with large enterprises; large firms often pay higher hourly wage rates than do small- and medium-sized firms." (Thompson, 1981, p. 274) (See, also, *Wall Street Journal*, 1989.) Of course, management may be able to temper the large firm's "overdog" handicap by astute (and costly) public relations management. Last, and possibly least, is the direct cost of each additional layer of management.

This review of the handicaps associated with increasing size of firm suggests a general hypothesis: *firms tend to grow until they become unmanageable.*

FIRM SIZE AND ACCOUNTING:
A SYMBIOSIS

The number and variety of possible explanations for limits on firm size, together with the somewhat general nature of each explanation, may leave one unconvinced of the precise nature of the fixity that supports indivisibility of coordination as a rationale for firms reaching a variety of size equilibria. Nevertheless, it is plausible that constraints on firm growth have been, and will continue to be, effective, and that one or more of the above factors have been involved. *To the extent that developments in accounting have mitigated such general constraints as bounded rationality, opportunism, information losses, control loss, and incentive dilution, it may have pushed out the upper bound on firm size, and thus brought economies of scale within reach.*

But more specific effects can be identified. The coordination indivisibility limitation is attacked directly by a budgeting system. Advocates of budgeting long have insisted that it contributes to planning, coordination, and control. The process of budgeting includes communication among functional divisions of a business, so that the right arm knows what the left arm is planning. Large businesses typically have formal budgetary planning systems. One part of that process is capital budgeting typically based on discounted cash flow analysis techniques that have become popular since World War II. To Kaldor's 1930 manager, comparisons of alternative investment projects was a time-consuming task for top management; now financial analysts and department managers provide a lot of (computer-processed) data supporting their recommendations.

The tendency of large firm management to suffer a loss of control is also mitigated by accounting techniques. Performance reports, based to varying degrees on the responsibility accounting notion and designed to fit the management hierarchy, are most prominent. Budgeting and standard costing are routinely involved. Performance reports that compare standard costs and/or budgeted numbers against actual numbers, and supported by staff or subordinate comments on variances, contribute substantially to the degree of control exercised by the chief executive officer of a large firm. Imagine the control loss such an executive would suffer if the outputs of the accounting department were unavailable for a few months! In sum, large size has made budgeting, project analysis techniques, standard costing, and many forms of performance reports valuable to firms, so has stimulated their development. At the same time, those accounting techniques have raised the upper bound on firm size.

Another plausible hypothesis regarding accounting and size is that accounting contributes to growth of firm size by providing financial information to investors who are willing to rely on it sufficiently to provide capital to the growing firm.

The influences run in both directions. Neither today's firms nor today's accounting methods could have developed without the other.[2]

60. *The tendency of increasing size of firm to challenge the bounds of human rationality (including memory) has stimulated the development of accounting for thousands of years.*

61. *The communication problems, control loss, coordination difficulties, and bureaucratic tendencies plaguing the managements of large firms have stimulated the evolution of control-oriented accounting procedures such as budgeting, standard costing, segment performance reporting, and variance analysis.*

62. *Because both motivation to work toward firm objectives and management's direct observability of individual performance are impaired as size of firm increases, accounting-based performance reports are more fully developed in large firms than in small ones.*

63. *As size of firm increases, opportunistic behavior and incentive dilution encourage managements to make greater use of internal control devices such as separation of duties and internal auditing.*

64. *Increasing specialization of labor in growing firms stimulates an interest in financial information about specialized activities and makes the gathering of cost and revenue data about those activities easier, thus leading to the development of finer classification of data on specific functions.*

65. *Development of more economical, high volume data processing equipment and techniques are partly attributable to large firms.*

66. *Accounting is valued more highly in large firms than in small firms.*

NOTES

1. For a contrary view, see Drucker (1989, p. 20).

2. The symbiosis of accounting and size of firm will remind accounting historians of another oft-quoted symbiosis:

> The characteristic pattern of business organization resulting from systematic bookkeeping has been of crucial importance for the development of capitalism in its most essential aspect. One cannot imagine what capitalism would be without double-entry bookkeeping; the two phenomena are connected as intimately as form and contents. One cannot say whether capitalism created double-entry bookkeeping, as a tool in its expansion, or whether perhaps, conversely, double-entry bookkeeping created capitalism. (Sombart, 1924/1953, p. 38)

CHAPTER 6
INTEGRATION, DIVERSIFICATION
AND ORGANIZATION

As compared with such underlying psycho-economic factors as bounded rationality and opportunistic behavior, a firm's size, its expansion strategy, and its organization structure are more intertwined with accounting. Bounded rationality and opportunism, for example, were observable before the existence of significant firms and accounting systems, but the latter two have developed together. In Chapter 5, I argued that growth in the size of firms influenced accounting and that accounting, in turn, had some influence on the maximum size of a viable firm. In this chapter, we find that the firm's expansion strategy and its form of organization also interact with accounting, each influencing the other.

Expansion strategy is addressed first. Aside from simple increase in the volume of given activities, firms typically consider "upstream," or backward integration, or "downstream," or forward integration, and/or they consider "horizontal" diversification of products sold. The two historically dominant forms of organization have been called "functional" and "multi-divisional," or M-form. The influence of these organization forms on accounting is addressed in the third section of the chapter. One might observe that all of the prominent firms in an economy are large, vertically integrated, and diversified. That makes separating the influences difficult. A good place to start is with a clear understanding of the underlying economic phenomena, especially vertical integration.

VERTICAL INTEGRATION

An integrated firm performs more than one activity, each of which is related to another or others by an output-input linkage. To integrate vertically means to extend the sequence of activities within a firm, either by adding an activity previously performed by a supplier (making instead of buying a good used in the firm) -- backward integration -- or by adding an activity previously performed by a customer of the firm -- forward integration. A state of integration exists when separable activities, such as mixing dough, baking, slicing and wrapping bread all occur in the same firm.

Certain integrations of activities, such as those just mentioned, are common and may, therefore, seem natural. James Thompson called such a set of activities "core technology" (1967, p. 19). Others, such as inclusion of wheat growing, flour milling, selling bread at retail, sandwich making, and sandwich retailing in a firm that mixes, bakes, slices and wraps bread, are less common. Lack of a market for the intermediate product, e.g., mixed, unbaked dough, suggests that adjacent activities commonly are integrated. Large firms that are not highly integrated are scarce or nonexistent. Practically speaking, all firms are integrated firms.

Now consider any two adjacent activities mentioned in the preceding two paragraphs, such as mixing bread dough and baking bread. It is possible to organize the related activities by administrative direction within one firm, and it is possible to organize them in two firms related by market transactions. Certain pairs of the above activities commonly are organized within one firm; others commonly are organized across markets. Why? According to Coase, "a firm will tend to expand until the costs of organizing an extra transaction within the firm become equal to the costs of carrying out the same transaction by means of an exchange on the open market or the costs of organizing in another firm." (1937, p. 395) This is a "transaction cost economics" answer to the integration question.

Williamson has a broader explanation: "Holding the nature of the good or service to be delivered constant, economizing takes place with reference to the sum of production and transaction costs, whence trade-offs in this respect must be recognized." (1985, p. 22) That is Williamson's answer to Coase's question: "Why is not all production carried on by one big firm?" (1937, p. 394) The socialist economy is a version of one big firm with centralized decision making; the common handicap of the two entities is discussed below.

Starting with a given extent of integration, certain circumstances may influence a firm's decision whether to integrate further or to "disintegrate" -- i.e., to add or drop any activity sequentially associated with the firm's present or retained activities. If accounting changes, or influences, any of those "integration circumstances," it may play a role in the organization of the firm, so the identification of integration circumstances is of interest to one concerned with the development of firm accounting. A listing of circumstances typically favoring integration and those typically favoring market organization may disclose those influencing, or influenced by, accounting.

Circumstances Typically Favoring Integration

These fall into three classes.

1.   Opportunities to save on transaction costs. According to Williamson (1985, pp. 85-86), the main purpose to be served by vertical integration is economizing on transaction costs.

        a) Contracting costs. Williamson emphasizes the likelihood of saving on contracting costs as well as control over the relationship when the supplier and user are in the same firm. For example, "the firm possesses a comparatively efficient conflict resolution machinery." (1971, p. 114) Blair and Kaserman argued that "internalization reduces the incentive to engage in opportunistic behavior (although) it does not reduce it altogether." (1983, p. 24) In general, internal relationships typically are less formal and more easily revised than are external contracts. As noted in an earlier section, the greater the asset specificity, the greater the saving on governance costs through internal organization.

b) Innovation.   Teece argues that innovation and integration of activities go together. Innovations are intellectual property that is hard to protect if the functions required to exploit it -- research and development, engineering, marketing, manufacturing -- reside in different firms. Furthermore, when there are significant interdependencies -- functionally or systemically (e.g., electronic funds transfer schemes, or a photographic innovation involving cameras, film, and development) introduction of an innovation will often result in differing benefits and costs to various parties. This effect makes it difficult if not impossible to coordinate the introduction of such an innovation. While a system of frictionless markets could overcome this problem -- the firms obtaining the benefits could compensate those incurring the costs so that the introduction of the innovation would not depend on the degree of integration in the industry -- it is commonly recognized that it may be extremely difficult to engineer a workable compensation agreement, in part because all relevant contingencies are not known when the contract would need to be drawn up (Teece, 1987, p. 27).   To the extent that innovation is an increasingly important feature of the firm landscape, a tendency towards organization of activities in integrated firms rather than in market relationships is to be expected.

c)   Measurement and other information costs. Barzel (1982, p. 41) has emphasized the cost of measuring a good's quality, and has suggested that integration is advantageous when input quality is accepted as a surrogate for output quality because those inputs are easily observed and controlled within the firm. Williamson (1971, p. 114) suggests that a firm "may resort to internalization on account of economies of information exchange. It is widely accepted, for example, that communication with respect to complex matters is facilitated by a common training and experience," "repeated interpersonal interactions" and sensitivity to "subtle nuances."

2.   Physical and other technical circumstances, such as various types of spoilage, including heat loss in metal working. There is not much of a market for molten steel. While "cheek-by-jowl" siting of separate firms can, in principle, make the transfer time equal to that between departments in one firm, in practice integration of a "core technology" typically is observed. One could argue that the reasons for such integration would, on close inspection, be found to fall under (1) above.

3.   Strategic circumstances related to degrees of competition, absorption of risks, control of intellectual property and so on.

Circumstances Typically Favoring Market Organization

Four points are of interest here.

1.   Considering shifts of activities from market organization to the firm, "equilibrium is reached when the saving of

transaction (pricing) costs incurred in the product market is equaled at the margin by the rising agency costs (also transaction costs) within an emerging 'factor market'." (Cheung, 1983, p. 18) Viewing transaction costs more broadly, certain categories (not necessarily limited to agency costs) will tend to increase with greater integration; others decrease.

2.   High-powered incentives.   Integration dilutes the incentives motivating the people involved. Consider two firms with five equal partners in each. Any cost saving or revenue enhancement accomplished through an individual's efforts rebound to his/her account to the extent of 20 percent. If the two firms merge, that figure is diluted to 10 percent. Or, if a one-owner firm is acquired by a large publicly-owned firm by issuance of shares, the previous sole proprietor then enjoys a small share of the results of his efforts as manager of his division within the large firm.

3.   Availability of price information for optimization decisions.   Here the concern is with "how-to-do-it" decisions -- what inputs to utilize in achieving an output -- and volume decisions. When each related activity is a separate firm, the costs of its inputs and the revenues from its outputs are observable market prices. In the integrated firm, with sequential activities, many of those inputs and outputs have no close counterpart outside the firm, so their values are indeterminate. That hinders management in making optimization decisions.

4.   Production cost differences. Market organization often permits economies of scale. If a firm uses 100 units per year, purchase from a manufacturer who makes 100,000 units per year may be economical.

A more complete analysis would address the variations in degrees of control exercised by the using activity over the supplying activity within each of the above legal relationships: integration and separate firms.

A review of the above analysis reveals two "integration circumstances" that could be closely involved with accounting: the high-powered incentives provided by market organization and the availability of price information for optimization decisions in unintegrated activities. Consider the matter of incentives. The practice of rewarding superior performance requires distinguishing superior from inferior performance. Management's ability to evaluate the performance of personnel working in an integrated activity is dependent on the availability of acceptable information on that performance. If the unit's inputs come from other in-firm activities and its outputs go to other in-firm activities, market prices for the unique intermediates being transferred are not observed. Hence, profitability of the integrated activity is not easily measured. If profit is the central goal of the firm, performance of managers at all levels must mean contribution to profit. One might hypothesize that high level managers in integrated firms would seek to counter "the loss in reliable performance measures that attends integration ..." (Holmstrum, 1988, p. 2) by either using highly reliable measures of poor definitions of performance (e.g., direct costs only) or less reliable measures of more carefully defined performance (e.g., return on investment based on allocations and estimates). A management that is successful in finding ways of measuring activity performance and rewarding activity managers might help the integrated firm compete with market organization of related activities, thus partially explaining the existence and growth of integrated firms. Demand for such measurements might have influenced the development of accounting in integrated firms.

The Role of Market Prices in Decisions

An understanding of the role of accounting numbers in the management of integrated firms may be enhanced by consideration of the role of market prices of goods (commodities and services) in decisions. To a *buyer*, a price provides information on the cost of obtaining the benefits the good can provide to him/her. To a *seller*, a price measures the benefits to be derived from a sale. The buyer must compare the market price with the anticipated benefits from buying and using the purchased good. The seller must compare the price with the anticipated sacrifices made by giving up other opportunities when selling the good. Thus, the buyer has a more objective measure of the cost side of the transaction, while a seller has a more objective measure of the benefit side - - the number of monetary units stated as the price.

One could object that the clearer view of one side of the transaction afforded by the money price is only an illusion. The actual benefit from receiving money is the benefit from having goods on which the money is spent, and that is just as subjective as the cost from giving up the good being sold. Similarly, the actual cost incurred in paying money is the sacrifice of the other goods that could have been purchased with that money. But experience suggests that people do accept the amount of money paid/received as a measure of the sacrifice/benefit involved in the transaction. Whether that acceptance is due to bounded rationality in relation to one's capacity to see through the money to the utility of "what could have been had instead," or to a subconscious acceptance of his/her own ability to equate the marginal benefits of alternative goods may not matter here. When a market price measures one side of a transaction, the actor considers himself/herself to be well-informed.

The transactions of a producing unit may now be considered. When the manager is deciding on the mix of inputs to be used in producing a product, the unit prices of those inputs must be known if production costs are to be minimized. Choices from among alternative materials, between more automatic equipment and less automatic equipment (with various labor-saving and power-using features) are not well-informed without unit prices of the alternative inputs. When the manager purchases those inputs in markets, the prices that must be paid in those markets are critical information. Similarly, decisions regarding commencing, continuing, or terminating production, and how much to produce require information regarding the values of outputs (as well as the costs of inputs). When the manager sells those outputs directly into markets, he/she is guided by market prices. The availability of market price information regarding inputs and outputs permits the manager of a single-activity firm to make classical economizing decisions and to compare performance across enterprises and periods.

Economizing in the Integrated Firm

Now compare the supply of information available to a manager of one activity in an integrated firm with that described above. Take the case of a manager of an activity who receives inputs from other activities within the firm: from a materials storeroom, a plant facilities management department, a personnel department, an "in-house' power plant, several parts fabricating departments, and so on. Similarly, the outputs of the activity in question are transferred to other in-firm activities, rather than to outside customers. In the absence of any special effort to supply such information, how does the activity manager know the unit values of inputs and outputs? He/she has no readily available number for the cost of using an hour of a certain labor skill, the cost of an hour of machine time, the cost of a kilowatt-hour of electricity or a pound of material produced by a previous activity within the firm. Nor does the manager know the value that anyone else sets on his/her activity outputs.   Economizing amounts to fumbling in the dark. Performance can only be measured in nonmonetary terms.

In a regime of perfect and complete markets, a manager of an intermediate activity within an integrated firm could observe market prices for the labor services provided by the firm's human resources management activity, for the raw materials provided to other activities by the firm's storeroom, for the subassemblies transferred between activities, and so on. But complete and perfect markets do not exist. In the absence of observable market prices for those *unique*, setting-specific goods, which have no exact counterparts in observable markets, activity managers seek estimates of such prices as measurements of the costs of using their inputs and values of their outputs. Such estimates have been called simulated market prices (Staubus, 1986) or quasi-prices (McCullers and McDill, 1970).

Accounting's Contributions *Economizing* in the Integrated Firm

Several major examples of numbers that are produced by accountants and used by managers as measures of intra-firm activity inputs and outputs may be listed.

1. Unit product costs, including partial unit costs (by departments, by cost elements) and complete costs of units transferred from a production activity to a sales activity, or to a separate division. (See H. T. Johnson's (1983) scenario describing the development of unit product costing when the putting-out system was replaced by the factory system in the English textile industry).
2. Unit noncost prices intended to represent values of transferor division's outputs and costs of transferee's inputs.
3. Aggregations of costs as in a department's monthly report showing costs of resources supplied to that department.
4. Inter-activity allocations of resource costs, e.g., from a "service" department to "producing" departments.

5.   Numbers on prospective increments and decrements in
          resource costs under alternative future courses of action,
          i.e., ad hoc costing for decisions.

With the exception of the second example listed above, those
accounting numbers typically are not described as estimates of
market prices of resources, but they do tend to serve as
surrogates for market prices when managers make technology,
volume, and performance judgments. Of course, certain crude
allocations, upon careful consideration, are regarded as
unsuitable measures of the value of a resource being transferred
among activities. But when those crude numbers are mixed
with more suitable numbers they may tend to be treated as
usable measures of resource transfers, especially in assessments
of managerial performance. In other words, the suitability for
economizing decisions of the numbers that accounting attaches
to transfers of resources within integrated firms varies a great
deal and is seen by those involved as varying. Accountants
have not given the measurement of activity costs and benefits
high priority.

The Integrated Firm and the Socialist Economy

          The parallel between the large integrated firm and the
socialist economy should now be apparent. Indeed, their
similarities, in various respects, have been recognized widely.
The point to be made here, however, is that in the absence of
special efforts, both systems suffer from the same handicap:
absence of relevant measurements of the costs and benefits of
actions undertaken. In the socialist economy the markets that
could provide prices measuring the costs and benefits of actions
are deliberately suppressed. In the integrated firm operating in
a "market economy," special efforts -- accounting practices --
must be made to simulate the unobservable market prices for
intrafirm transfers among integrated activities.

It should be apparent that terms such as relevant measurements, poor prices, and suboptimization relate to the objectives of the economic unit under analysis. Externalities are overlooked. In this context, an externality is a cost or benefit caused by an economic unit's actions that does not fall on that economic unit. Those externalities -- individual, activity, firm, or economy externalities -- are overlooked here in the conventional way. One is inclined to assume, in 1995, that prices set by socialist planners and by bureaucrats in firm headquarters typically -- but not always -- are less satisfactory as measures of social costs and benefits than are competitive market prices, despite externalities.

Integration: Conclusions and Propositions

The organization of a series of sequential activities within one integrated firm instead of in several firms connected by market transactions robs activity managers of much of the market price information regarding their inputs and outputs. When the "visible hand" of management (Chandler, 1977) replaces the invisible hand of market forces, it is guided (how well?) by information from a different source: accounting. That system is in an early stage of its evolution.

Despite continuing impressive evidence of the success of economic systems guided by market prices, compared to the failures of socialist systems, we do recognize that market prices are not always perfect guides. Nevertheless, those imperfect market prices are recognized as the standard against which accounting's substitutes are compared.[1] The accounting numbers developed in integrated firms for use as substitutes for market prices of activity inputs and outputs may be evaluated as such,, i.e. as surrogates for setting-specific market prices.[2] They are more likely to measure up if they are consciously designed to do so. To the extent that the accounting numbers fail to simulate setting-specific market prices, economic decisions by managers of activities within integrated firms will fail to achieve the efficiencies described by the competitive markets model.

The above reasoning leads to the following hypotheses regarding potential impacts of accounting in integrated firms:

1.   In the context of social welfare, the contributions that market prices make to efficiency might be replicated within the integrated firm by accounting numbers designed to estimate the unobservable market prices of activity inputs and outputs.

2.   The cost and value of accounting measurements of activity inputs and outputs in vertically integrated firms are factors in determining the extent of integration and the size of integrated firms in an economy. For an integrating step to take place, the cost savings in other transaction costs and production costs must more than offset the losses from the information inferiority of accounting prices compared to market prices of resources and products.

3.   The absence of observable market prices for the unique goods transferred among activities within the integrated firm reduces the efficiency of the firm in the same way that reliance on nonmarket prices reduces the efficiency of a socialist economy.

The influence of the integration feature of firms on the development of accounting is summarized in two propositions -- one quite hypothetical, the other more descriptive:

67.   *The incremental role for accounting when several activities are organized in one integrated firm is to supply managers with estimates of the costs of inputs to, and the values of outputs from the specific activities that constitute segments of the integrated firm's total activities.   Accountants   have   resisted   that conceptualization of their role.*[3]

68.   *Although integration has not convinced accounting explicitly and systematically to accept the role of providing surrogates for market prices of activity inputs and outputs, it has stimulated progress toward accounting for intra-firm events through such devices as "cost accounting," segment performance reports, transfer pricing, and ad hoc analyses for "make-or-buy" (backward integration) decisions and "sell-or-process-further" (forward integration) decisions.*

The contrast between these two propositions suggests an intriguing potential development in accounting. What environmental changes would be required for that potential to be realized?

DIVERSIFICATION

Diversification is an alternative to vertical integration as an expansion strategy for the firm, although the two are by no means mutually exclusive. When a portion of the output of one product is used as an input to another product of the firm, the two activities are integrated. Economizing and accounting in that circumstance has been discussed above. Here we concentrate on diversification alone.

Diversification of products is primarily a twentieth century development in the economics of the firm. Richard Rumelt dates the movement from 1949. Twenty-five years later, he could write: "the dominant form of large business enterprise in the United States today is the diversified multidivisional corporation." (Rumelt, 1974, p. 154)

Rationales for diversification have been given a good deal of attention by writers such as Rumelt and David Teece (1980). For the present purpose, five such rationales are significant:

1. The portfolio risk idea -- investing in a number of products with small covariance of their sales contributes to stability of firm performance.
2. To take advantage of decentralized (M-form) organizational structure. Those who see decentralization of decision making and profit center reporting as providing great opportunities to evaluate performance, offer effective incentives, develop managerial capabilities, and allocate capital to its best uses may prefer to invest in and/or manage a diversified firm, because a decentralized organizational structure works best with diversification of products.
3. Economics of scope. Teece (1980, pp. 224-227) argues that the sharing of a factor input by more than one product yields savings from producing the products in the same firm, but only if that factor cannot be divided and portions sold for use by other firms. Teece suggests that know-how and specialized, indivisible physical assets fit that description.
4. Loss of confidence in the future of existing products.
5. Empire building -- efforts by managements to enlarge their domains.

A review of the five rationales for diversification listed above suggests that the second is the one most likely to involve accounting; that involvement will be considered below under M-form organization.

The significance of diversification to accounting may depend somewhat on the definition of diversification. While a firm may diversify its sources of supply, locations of production facilities, types of customers, and so on, the most interesting type of diversification in the present context is in products sold. In manufacturing firms, production of multiple products in the same plant poses the product cost accounting problem. (With one product, its unit cost is total cost divided by number of units.) It seems safe to say that the set of techniques known as product cost accounting -- employing the direct/indirect cost distinction, allocation methods, work-in-process accounts, classification of costs by cost elements, and so on -- was developed in response to the needs of managers in multiple products firms.

Diversification may impact accounting less directly through its effects on management's reliance on written communication, especially financial reports, as opposed to more direct, less formal sources of information. A manager with long experience in a specific product division may be able to rely heavily on his/her direct, informal sources of information about its operations, whereas a manager recently transferred from another product division must depend more on financial reports. A top manager who came up through product division X is likely, according to this line of reasoning, to rely more on financial reports for evaluating division Y than he/she does for evaluating division X. In general, with a large number of product divisions, top management is not expert in the activities of those divisions, so depends more on accounting to provide comparable information for performance evaluation and control. This has been called "managing by the numbers" by Harold Geneen, CEO of the widely diversified IT&T during the late 1960s and 1970s (Geneen, 1984). One might, therefore, hypothesize that as between a 10,000 persons, one-product firm and a 10,000 persons, 20-product firm, the latter's top management will make greater use of accounting information.

69.   *The production of multiple products in one plant obscures product cost data, so multiproduct plants tend to develop more refined systems for measuring product costs than do single-product plants.*

70.   *Diversification increases management's dependence on accounting reports because managers in diversified firms have less personal experience with the operations they manage than do managers in single product firms.*

FORM OF ORGANIZATION

Only the two traditional forms of organization -- functional and multidivisional -- are discussed here. Matrix and network forms, for example, are passed over because their incremental influences on the development of accounting are not clear. Similarly, recent developments in types of relationships among separately owned entities that challenge customary concepts of boundaries of a firm are not addressed.

Functional (U) Form of Organization

Firms are said to be organized on a functional basis (in a unitary form) when the organization chart and the realities of managerial responsibilities emphasize business functions such as manufacturing, marketing, finance and, either on their own or under another function, activities such as human resource management, engineering, research and development, purchasing, and accounting. That form of organization was dominant in American manufacturing companies until at least the middle of the twentieth century (Rumelt, 1974, p. 63). It contrasts with the multidivisional (M) form of organization structure.

The heads of a firm's functional departments have no direct responsibility for achieving any particular level of profit, as profit is not associated with their departments. They live and breath the specific goals and problems of their departments, usually involving such matters as quality, volume of output, personnel issues, and cost minimization. Marketing people are vitally concerned with unit and dollar volume of sales and, presumably, selling costs, but not profits as such. Only the very top executives focus on profit as their "bottom line." Departmental planning and control does not involve profit, because departments are cost centers or revenue centers, but not profit centers. Instead, cost and sales budgets are established, standard costs might be set, and performance is evaluated by comparing actual results against those budgets and standards.

The Multidivisional (M-Form) of Organization

Variations and borderline cases are common, but the standard M-form organization structure divides the firm into product divisions and then subdivides those divisions into functional departments. Each product division is a "profit center," in the sense that an operating statement is prepared for it showing its revenues, expenses and some version of profit or contribution to unallocated costs and profit. Product division managers buy and sell their inputs and outputs in transactions with "outsiders" at market prices and in interdivisional transfers at surrogates for market prices, thus putting them in intimate touch with that paragon of economic information sources: markets. Product divisions may be combined into product groups at a higher level if there are too many to report directly to a headquarters executive. General Electric, for example, has approximately 150 profit centers that are grouped into 26 "businesses", excluding financial industry businesses.

The multidivisional form of organization often is associated with decentralization, or pushing decision-making authority down the organization chart. Vancil puts the emphasis on decentralization of authority for profit-oriented decisions as opposed to purely technical decisions. "Decentralized firms are commonly referred to as employing the 'divisional' form of organization, in contrast to centralized firms which employ the 'functional' form." (1978, p. 2) Holmstrum emphasizes the relationship between extent of delegation and quality of performance measurements: "the agent's flexibility will be more restricted the poorer the performance measures are." (1988, p. 13) Chandler dates the earliest use of the product-division form of organization in the United States from the 1920s (1962, p. 44) Rumelt (1986, p. 65) estimated that, by 1949, 20 percent of the largest 500 U.S. industrial companies were organized in product divisions, and that this share increased to 76 percent by 1969. Distribution, financial, and other service companies, which often do not have product divisions, typically have other units that are treated as profit centers, such as geographical divisions. For the present purpose, the term "M-form firm" will be used to include them as well as product-division firms.

The M-form organization structure is intimately related to a diversification strategy. The two go together so well that distinguishing cause and effect is difficult. As was suggested under *Diversification* above, certain firms may have chosen the diversification route to growth because it permitted use of the multidivisional form, whereas growth through either forward or backward integration restrained the firm from enjoying the advantages of profit centers if relevant market prices of intermediate products were not observable for use as transfer prices. Chandler's general conclusion (1962, p. 14) that (organizational) structure follows (diversification/integration) strategy may not be entirely true.

U-form and M-form firms differ greatly in their uses of financial information. In motivation of managers through incentives, U-form firms do not emphasize profit (except for a very few top managers), do not evaluate and reward most managers based on profit, so may not be as successful in achieving profit as an otherwise comparable divisionalized (M-form) firm would. U-form firms might also be handicapped by poor optimization decisions related to specific firm activities. If there are well-established markets for the firm's intermediate products, but the firm ignores prices in those markets because it recognizes no "profit centers" and, therefore, no intersegment transfers, but only passes costs on to succeeding departments, it passes up opportunities to use the market's wisdom. Both technology (how-to-do-it) and volume decisions are likely to be made on the bases of measurements that are poor surrogates for market values of the inputs and outputs of those specific activities, thus handicapping U-form firms in competition with

M-form firms.   Of course, for M-form firms to have such advantages, they must in fact utilize market price information (or reasonable surrogates therefore) in their optimization decisions.

In sum, U-form firms' failure to take advantage of market prices in measuring inputs and outputs other than on the total firm basis may handicap them in the areas of motivation of personnel and optimization decisions.   Therefore, one might predict that M-form firms would dominate U-form firms where both forms of organization are feasible.   Also, the size of U-form firms (with no profit center accounting or market oriented transfer pricing) would seem to be limited as the benefits of market-based measurements are lost to the management hierarchy of the growing firm.   On the other hand, the future of large U-form firms may not be so bleak;   it is possible that accounting will develop means of measuring the inputs and outputs of narrow activities so as to provide better information for evaluating performance of activities and their managers and for optimization decisions.

In many cases, unfortunately, firms have not been able to find acceptable surrogates for market prices for interactivity transfers.   The typical proprietary product, such as a cosmetic or an automobile, is transferred from manufacturing to sales at some version of cost that is not intended to provide for measurements of activity profits.   Cost center accounting prevails. Thus, the absence of market-related price information prevents use of the M-form organizational structure.

Turning to problems facing growing firms that were recognized in Chapter 5, the "management problems," starting with coordination, that were viewed as diseconomies of firm scale might be at least somewhat mitigated by use of the M-form of organization. The overwhelming task of coordinating the various functions in a large firm can be made manageable by splitting it among several division general managers. Each of them can coordinate the various functions and makes choices from among alternatives facing his/her division, leaving a much smaller set of decisions to the top management. In other words, coordination need not be a fixed, indivisible factor; it can be expanded by use of division coordinators.

The control loss problem and information losses in transmission are mitigated by dividing the firm into several, much smaller firms with fewer hierarchical layers, as can the problem of incentive erosion due to dilution of cost and benefit incidence and lack of job satisfaction in large firms. Bureaucratic costs, too, appear to be reducible by breaking up a large firm into manageable parts that have many -- though not all -- of the attributes of small businesses. In sum, the major sources of diseconomies of firm scale might be mitigable by use of the M-form organization structure, thus permitting large firms to enjoy some of the advantages of Marshall's "small employer." In general, the more complicated and varied the business (e.g., number of products, locations, technology, marketing channels, government relations) the smaller (in revenues) the size limit for a firm organized functionally and the more likely the firm is to adopt the profit center form of organization and accounting. Thus, the product division form of organization tends to dominate the functional form in diversified firms.

One other contribution of the multidivisional form of organization that was mentioned under diversification was to make it feasible to allocate capital among the several "businesses" within the firm based on their performance. M-form firms generally attempt to shift capital from mature, "cash cow" businesses to growth areas. The prerequisite information on the profitability of the firm's several businesses is not readily available under the unitary form of organization.

The advantages of the multidivisional form of organization that have been mentioned above should not lead one to believe that all problems facing firms can be solved by adoption of an M-form organization structure. The product divisions are not exactly small businesses with all of the advantages of small businesses, together with the advantages of being members of a large firm. Division general managers must be controllable by headquarters management; they are not sole proprietors running their own show. Also, it is possible to lose a major advantage of integrated vs. market organization of activities -- more cooperative relationships among activity managers -- if division managers are given such strong incentives that they become motivated to help their own divisions at the expense of other divisions with whom they "do business" -- the old problem of "department centeredness" pointed out by Argyris long ago (1953, p. 105). A new task of top management in M-form firms is resolving differences among divisions.

The success and popularity of the multidivisional form of organization in recent decades and major developments in accounting go hand-in-hand. Profit center (and investment center) reporting, use of purposefully developed transfer prices, and emphasis on return on investment and residual income in divisional planning and reporting have been employed to attack some of the most painful symptoms of large firm size, including control loss, lack of coordination, incentive erosion, bureaucratic tendencies, and other consequences of bounded rationality and unbounded self-interest. Within its limitations, "managing by the numbers" has reached its highest development in the very large multidivisional firm.

71. *Replacement of the functional form of organization by the multidivisional form in many large firms has encouraged development of profit center reporting, transfer pricing techniques, and emphasis on return on investment and, to a limited extent, residual income.*

72. *A firm is not likely to adopt profit center accounting if interactivity transfers are not measurable by close surrogates for observable market prices.*

Concluding Note

The observations of an economist (Tullock, 1965) not known for his work on business management are surprisingly consistent with the conclusions reached in Chapters 5 and 6.

The supervisory function of cost accounting ... appears to have been a decisive factor in shaping the structure of large corporate hierarchies. (p. 199)

Cost accounting is the best known technique for supervision, and modern industrial civilization very largely depends upon it. (p. 202)

The accounts of an organization do not, of course, measure the performance of the separate divisions of the hierarchy with complete accuracy. (p. 201)

... (T)here is no simple way of valuing (outputs that) are not directly priced.

[Managements] must reach decisions as to the relative efficiency of certain divisions that do not produce outputs that are directly marketable. It should always be recognized that these decisions are based on less accurate information than in the cases where prices are readily available. It is, therefore, technically impossible to administer a large organization, the various divisions of which perform successive operations on the same product, with as high degree of accuracy as one of similar size that is organized into divisions producing discrete products.

This analysis, if correct, resolves one of the minor mysteries of economics. It has always seemed probable that economies of scale resulting from larger and larger productive processes would lead to large companies growing steadily larger with the small companies being destroyed. This has not occurred.

If the economies of scale are a significant factor, it seems clear that some countervailing factor must be present that prevents these corporate giants from taking advantage of them. The intrinsic limitations on accounting as a means of supervision provide this factor. (p. 205)

NOTES

1. Cf. the large body of research in which securities market response is accepted as partial evidence of the quality of accounting information, despite many disclaimers.

2. The concept of simulating setting-specific market prices for intra-firm stocks and flows, based on accepted principles of market economics, was explained in Staubus, 1986. For example, markets are observed to value prospective cash flows, to allow for the probability of those cash flows occurring, to allow for risk, to reflect current costs, and to respond to supply and demand variations in submartingale patterns that leave prices at one date correlated with the most recent earlier prices, thus supporting the use of recent "historical costs" as surrogates for current prices. Although accountants tend to reflect those principles of market economics in their measurements, there are important exceptions.

3. The interested reader may wish to trace the ancestry of this proposition through Staubus (1971, chapter 2; 1986, pp. 118-120; 1988, p. 250) as well as in other references cited therein.

CHAPTER 7
VALUELESS ACCOUNTING: WHY?

The previous chapters of this book seem to explain many features of current accounting practice in countries based on West European traditions. They have not, however, specifically addressed the most persistent controversy in that accounting: Should the originally recorded, transaction-based prices of assets and liabilities be updated for reporting in a set of financial statements? In practice the "old-measurement" solution is most generally accepted, with some modest exceptions. Many believe it is justified by conservatism. At this point, one might reasonably ask: Do the explanations for current accounting practices provided in this book support the old-measurements solution? If not, a long shadow is cast over the value of those explanations, or "influences shaping the development of accounting in firms."

This chapter originally was written for a conference presentation and not to illustrate the theme of the book. The style differs; perhaps that makes it a more independent test of the theme, because the objective has not been to support the theme, but to answer the question: Why does valueless accounting prevail?

VALUELESS ACCOUNTING

Anyone who has kept in touch with the major accounting policy debates in English-speaking countries in recent decades is aware of the tremendous resistance that appears whenever a proposal is made to switch from some version of "historical cost" to a more up-to-date measurement of any category of asset. Proposals to up-date measurements of liabilities encounter similar resistance. For the sake of convenience of expression, the liability issue often is ignored in this chapter, but it is included in the subject.

In colloquial terms, the argument is between historical cost and current value. However, to reduce the issue to its essence, it can be limited to the choice between old and current measurements, where current means "as of the balance sheet date," and old means "at acquisition date" in the case of an asset and "when incurred" in the case of a liability. The term "value" could be omitted in stating the issue, but since many of the combatants see a battle between cost and value, use of the term "value" may help to communicate the essence of the argument. But cost does not apply to liabilities, so a broader term is needed. The opposite of value accounting is valueless accounting, so those terms are used here to apply to both assets and liabilities in preference to the awkward expressions "current measurements accounting" and "old measurements accounting."

Another clarification might be worthwhile. Acceptance of the double entry convention and the comprehensive concept of income ties asset and liability values to income. That is, if income is the change in net assets, failure to record the changes in net asset values is a failure to record income. We do have examples of the recording of value changes in balance sheet accounts without reporting them on the income statement, but the reverse is hard to imagine. Without value accounting, there is no income accounting. Valueless accounting is profitless accounting.

This discussion, however, does not focus on the argument between cost and value. Rather, it is addressed to the question: Why does valueless accounting prevail over major sectors of the U.S. economy? One answer, recognizing that accounting practices are chosen by people, is that those with the power to choose like it. That brings up two obvious questions:

Who has the power to choose? Why do they like it? An indirect answer to the first question was given in Chapter 4. The second question is the focal point of this chapter.

Two premises are relied upon: (1) Individuals value information on their wealth and income, including the wealth and income of any business they wholly or partially own. (2) Valueless accounting prevails with respect to major asset and liability categories in most industries in most industrial countries. Juxtaposition of these two premises frame the issue: If information on wealth and income is valued, why is it not provided routinely in enterprise financial statements? Rejection of either premise erases the issue.[1]

The bulk of the chapter consists of statements of several *hypotheses* each of which might partially explain the prevalence of valueless accounting. Support is offered for each hypothesis.

WHY IS VALUELESS ACCOUNTING PRACTICED?

Social scientists are accustomed to seeking reasons for what exists -- to searching for explanations. There must be a reason! Or reasons! It seems unlikely that evidence can be found that will convince everyone concerned -- or that even a majority would agree on the primary explanation. But it may be possible to illuminate the issue to a modest degree. To those seeking to understand why accounting is what it is, the lack of efforts to answer the question posed here is disturbing. Perhaps a crude effort to suggest answers will stimulate others to contribute additional evidence -- to add pieces to the puzzle.[2]

Conflict of Interests

Two possible explanations of valueless accounting are based on the presence of conflicts among the interests of firm constituents. They are the control function explanation and the management preference explanation.

The Control Function Explanation.-- The various constituent groups that deal with a business enterprise have conflicting interests; each wants to maximize its own benefits from doing business with the firm. Other things remaining equal, the larger the payoff to one party, the less someone else gets. Exactly what tactics are fair, ethical, honest, or legal is not always clear, but we do understand that the power of self-interest pushes parties across these lines from time to time. That tendency to behave "opportunistically" produces a need for controls, including the set of techniques known as accounting. To some, accounting's contributions to control are its *raison d'être*. One of the pillars of accounting control is documentary support; ideally, every formal entry in the books is supported by a document such as an invoice, a check, a time card, a deposit slip, or a materials requisition.

Dealings between "the firm' and other parties are called transactions. Each transaction is supported by some document which can, if necessary, be verified by checking with the other party. It is difficult to falsify documents supporting transactions, and auditors have a lot of experience in finding such falsifications. A write-down, however, could "explain" the misappropriation of an asset. A write-up could offset it just as well. Those entries would not be supported by documents originating outside the accounting department. "Transaction-based accounting" supported by documents involving other parties is a tight control system that should not be tampered with. Better to neglect the wealth measurement function, which can only be done poorly at best, than to risk breaching the control system. *Control is the primary function of accounting, and that function can be fulfilled better if revaluations are avoided.*

Providing the Qualities Management Prefers in Financial Reports.-- Valueless accounting contributes to the two qualities that management prizes the most: stability of reported earnings and the flexibility/control feature that permits "management" of the amounts reported for various income statement line items (Staubus, 1985, pp. 60-68). The contribution of valueless accounting to earnings stability is the easiest to explain. The most pejorative terms that managers responding to the Financial Accounting Standards Board can use about a proposed accounting method is "yo-yo accounting." Any method that is believed to result in wide swings in earnings is anathema to management, because it prevents them from meeting their earnings target and implies a lack of management control. Market prices of assets typically fluctuate, especially if the market is highly competitive, such as those for securities and graded commodities. When a management adopts "mark-to-market" accounting, it puts itself at the mercy of the market, rather than maintaining control over earnings. Managements hate yo-yo accounting and value accounting.

In an uncertain world, managements cannot have perfect control over reported earnings; they are affected by many unpredictable and uncontrollable events, many of which hurt earnings. It is highly desirable for managers to have the power to control at least a few line items to at least a moderate extent. This flexibility/control feature of an accounting method is prized by managers. To be buffeted by the whims of markets feels like riding a hang glider in a cyclone. The allowance method of accounting for uncollectible accounts, provisions for product warranties, self-insurance accounting, and expensing only cash contributions to pension plans have all been helpful to managers at times. But the feature of GAAP that makes the greatest contribution to management's control over reported earnings may well be historical cost (and historical proceeds for liabilities), including retention of old physical measurements, as in the cases of growing timber and hydrocarbon discoveries.

Note that those old values are helpful to management in this regard only if they differ from current values; their value to management depends on their failure to measure wealth at the reporting date. It is the reservoir of instant earnings stored in the undervaluations of assets and overvaluations of liabilities and the instant losses stored in the overvaluations of assets and undervaluations of liabilities that can, under certain circumstances, be called upon to adjust the period's earnings towards management's target. These reservoirs of instant earnings and instant losses are especially valuable if there is little cost, in the form of transaction costs or loss of service, incurred by selling the assets, or extinguishing the debt. Investment securities can play that role perfectly, so one should expect managements to fight to retain historical cost accounting for that asset category. Picking assets with unrealized gains (or losses) to sell in order to manipulate reported earnings has been called "cherry picking;" the right to pick cherries is prized by managements.

Historical cost for operating assets such as inventories and plant assets is also helpful. As long as nominal dollar accounting (without inflation adjustments) is in use, revaluations require reporting holding gains and losses, which presumably are to be disclosed (on their own line in the income statement if material) as opposed to being buried in lines such as cost of goods sold and depreciation. Over the last fifty years or so, the prices of most physical assets have trended upward, so any revaluations would tend to record gains. But with historical cost accounting, instead of reporting those gains on a separate line where they would be visible to all readers, who might attribute them to exogenous influences, holding gains are not isolated; they reduce cost of goods sold and depreciation, so readers are unable to "pull them out" and treat them as exogenous. Historical cost accounting has a liberal effect on the calculation of operating profit. Managements would be foolish to discard that advantage. Valueless accounting is far preferable to value accounting.

In sum, valueless accounting is of great assistance to managements as they seek their goal of reporting steadily rising earnings. Since most of today's accounting principles, especially the widespread adherence to historical cost, were chosen by managements, *an explanation for valueless*

*accounting is that managements like it for its contribution to
stability of earnings and liberal calculations of operating profit
and for the control over earnings reporting that it gives them.*
He who controls the information system can be expected to use
it to his own advantage.

Reliability Concerns

The term is used here in accordance with the American
definition (FASB, 1980) which includes verifiability, neutrality
and representational faithfulness. It can be said at the outset
that the explanatory power of the reliability hypothesis -- that
valueless accounting is viewed as more reliable than value
accounting -- varies a great deal across asset and liability items,
as the loss of reliability from revaluations varies a great deal.
One might argue that essentially no reliability is lost by
updating the values of listed or otherwise heavily traded
securities, whereas reliability clearly can suffer when the values
of work-in-process and finished goods inventories are updated,
and it is seriously impaired when obsolescent assets that are no
longer being produced are revalued.

Adhering to the limitation suggested in the introduction
-- including only the dating of measurements in the issue --
updating the historical costs of nonmonetary assets means using
current cost, not switching to exit value. In the cases of work-
in-process and finished goods inventories, that would mean
using current buying prices of inputs such as materials and
labor. It would also mean using the input quantities that were
required "historically." The unreliable features of product cost
accounting would continue, and reliability would be impaired
by substituting prices not supported by transaction documents
for transaction-based prices. On the other hand, the
manipulation opportunities permitted by the last-in, first-out cost
flow assumption would be lost. To repeat, the degree of
impairment of reliability clearly would vary a great deal across
the whole range of assets, and liabilities, that presumably would

be revalued in comprehensive value accounting. Therefore, one can reasonably conclude that valueless accounting is, in many cases, more reliable.

Another way to think about the reliability hazards in value accounting is to consider the interplay with conflicts of interests. Without tight documentary support for entries, those individuals who have both a special interest to promote and the opportunity to influence the accounting process might act opportunistically. Neutrality is one of the components of reliability. Given the freedom to choose from among alternatives, the biased individual can be expected systematically to lean in a particular direction, thus influencing the financial reports. This can be called manipulation. One conflict of interest that was noted above is that between owners and management when they are not the same parties. Thus, owners value reliability in management's financial reporting. Another conflict is between owner-managers and other parties, such as creditors. The latter also are understood to value reliability as a characteristic of financial information. In both of these cases, managers appear not to be the ones concerned about reliability; they are more likely to be the manipulators than the "manipulatees." But owners and creditors would appear to be concerned, so could be against value accounting on reliability grounds. Auditors, too, could favor transaction-based accounting on auditability (reliability) grounds.

Reliability, then, is a reasonable criterion on which to prefer valueless accounting. Its importance must vary across constituent groups, with absentee owners, creditors, and auditors appearing to have sound reasons for such a preference. It is not obvious, however, that managers have a basis for counting unreliability against value accounting for external reporting, although they could consider it a problem in internal performance evaluation because subordinate managers might behave opportunistically in choosing values.

Cost

To management, the cost involved in value accounting is measured in staff time. To the accounting staff, value accounting means work. To those not familiar with updating procedures, the perceived work is the first time work, and it can, no doubt, be substantial. But that's not all. Surely there would be additional work involved in updating values at every reporting date. After all, the old values are already there -- in the books. The updating work would be entirely incremental, in many applications. Of course, it is true that some of the work required for updating inventory values is routinely done when applying the lower-of-cost-and-market rule, and it is unlikely that managers of a securities portfolio would not monitor its current value. Nevertheless, finding current measurements of many assets and liabilities involves extra work. This can be thought of as the two-sets-of-books problem as long as income taxation is based on historical transactions.

The costs of updating values may have an especially strong influence on the views of those who have no feel for the benefits. The burdens are likely to be felt by the accounting staff who must do the work and by the financial management personnel whose budgets and skills are strained, while the benefits from value accounting accrue to external parties. (Operating managers presumably keep current on their costs without the aid of a formal system and without waiting for reporting dates.) The ultimate incidence of accounting costs may be on owners, if those costs cannot be passed on to customers, so they could prefer transaction-based accounting for that reason, if they are not impressed with the benefits. Surely *it is reasonable for accounting and financial management personnel, in particular, as well as top management whose operating results would be charged with the costs, to prefer valueless accounting because of its cost.*

Minimizing the Cost of Volatility

This point can be outlined as follows:

1.   Valueless accounting permits the smoothing of reported earnings by selectively picking the ripe and rotten cherries -- instant earnings and losses.
2.   Smooth earnings lead to stability of share prices (low beta).
3.   Smooth earnings and stable share prices lead to higher average share prices and lower costs of both debt and equity capital, because risk and return are correlated; these are benefits to shareholders.
4.   Two more speculative considerations might add weight to this explanation:
     a) Managers may feel more strongly than shareholders about earnings declines for two reasons: (i) Earnings reports are grade reports on managers' performance, so they are more sensitive than the less personally involved shareholders, and (ii) managers typically are less diversified than shareholders. Thus, managers are exposed to more risk than shareholders.
     b) Managers and certain less experienced shareholders may be so accustomed to emphasizing price-earnings ratios using earnings reports that mix the effects of changing prices with operating margins that they assume that earnings volatility caused by including holding gains and losses will cause share price changes instead of changes in the P/E multiple. (This point presumably does not apply to financial industries where securities gains and losses customarily are disclosed, so investors are accustomed to evaluating them separately from operating margins.)

It follows that valueless accounting can reduce the adverse effects of earnings volatility on cost of capital.

Permits Managers to Hold More Risky Assets

Value accounting would require reporting in income all fluctuations in values of assets (and liabilities) held. The resulting volatility of net income would upset risk-averse investors. Management necessarily would anticipate that response, so would switch to less volatile assets, contrary to the interests of investors. With valueless accounting, managements are able to obscure volatility, so they can hold a more risky portfolio and earn the accompanying higher returns. Valueless accounting gives management credit for the greater returns associated with risk without charging it for the risk. Investors would disapprove if they knew the risks managements were taking but "they don't know what's good for them." Contrary to the explanation above under "Minimizing the Cost of Volatility," managers are less concerned about risk than investors. *Valueless accounting is preferred because it permits managements more fully to achieve investors' wealth maximization objective.*

The riskiness of assets held is of concern to creditors as well. To them, the net worth buffer on the balance sheet may be just as important as net income. Consider the case of highly leveraged financial institutions such as banks and insurance companies. If they hold volatile assets that are not offset by liabilities of similar volatility and amount, the reporting of current values could show severely impaired capital -- even negative net worth in extreme cases. Recent experience with American savings and loan associations illustrates the point. If changes in market values had to be shown on balance sheets and income statements, financial institutions could not hold such volatile assets because the resulting financial statements would frighten creditors, such as depositors and policy holders, to the extent that a "run" could develop, thus destroying the institution.

When value changes are not reported so boldly, creditors are not frightened.

Also, regulators pay a lot of attention to capital ratios. If declines in asset values reduce capital below the required level, regulators may either choose to, or be required by law to take over and merge or liquidate the institution. That risk could only be avoided by matching the maturities of those assets and liabilities that would be subject to revaluation, i.e., by hedging the risk taken on one side of the balance sheet with an opposite risk on the other side. *Valueless accounting permits financial institutions to hold more risky assets that yield higher returns to the benefit of both creditors and owners.*

Owners' and Creditors' Conservatism

The conservatism doctrine that is taught in nearly all financial accounting textbooks has been explained as originating as a response of bankers to the natural optimism of managers. Absentee owners may be inclined to respond similarly. Managers' interests conflict with those of bankers and owners. In general, capitalists may tend to be a conservative lot who are reluctant to count their chickens before they are hatched. Perhaps their views are responsible for the general acceptance of lower-of-cost-and-market values in reporting current assets, the realization principle, and adherence to cost for noncurrent assets during a long period of generally rising prices. *Is this an explanation for valueless accounting?*

Experience with Write-ups

According to accounting lore, a number of U.S. companies recorded increases in values of nonmonetary assets in the 1920s and "lived to regret it" in the 1930s. The risk that managers who do so now would "end up with mud on their faces" is just not worth taking. Having "been burned once," it will be a long time before American managements try it again.

(The colorful metaphors have been chosen to help convey the strong feelings that drove a generation of financial managers.) A related expression, perhaps not literally true, is: "No one ever got sued for understating profits or owners' equity!" In more technical terms, the parties involved with financial reporting face an asymmetric loss function. Overstatements are recognized as potentially more damaging than are understatements. This view can not be given its proper weight without thinking of the chronological juxtaposition of the great depression and the freezing of accounting principles in place at the commencement of the standards-setting era in approximately 1939. *Is this a reason why old measurements are reported in American financial statements?*

Technological Progress and Accounting Regress

Evidence abounds that the pace of technological progress has accelerated throughout recent centuries, if not through history. That progress is accompanied by uncertainty as to the lives of many tangible and intangible assets, e.g. marketing programs, training. Intellectual property has become relatively more significant in markets' valuations of firms. Thus, one can argue that off-balance sheet assets play larger roles than in the past and that the lives and service patterns of balance sheet assets are less accurately estimated. Liabilities may be in trouble too; the litigious society has increased firms' off-balance sheet liabilities. If one accepts this fading picture of modern accounting, one might easily be discouraged from emphasizing accounting measurement in general. Why bother with value accounting when accounting is so poor anyway? *The hypothesis here is that accounting has been discouraged from updating measurements by the increasing failures of accounting associated with rapid changes in environmental circumstances.*

Income Taxation

Two hypotheses can be used to support the idea that income taxation explains the preference for valueless accounting. One is that the goal of saving and postponing taxes has so dominated the thinking of those concerned with income measurement that any accounting method that typically results in lower income is intuitively preferred over the alternative method. With a long-term trend towards rising prices, old measurements are preferable to more current ones. The second hypothesis is that a more liberal method of computing income for general financial reporting must not be introduced because the tax law writers might thereby be influenced to put it into the internal revenue code. Experience with Statement of Financial Accounting Standards No. 34, Capitalization of Interest Cost (1979), supports this concern. *Income tax considerations lead to a preference for old measurements.*

Explanations Related to Auditing

Auditors' interest in verifiability was mentioned above under reliability. Three other possible explanations relate to auditing.

Auditors' Ties to Management.-- This point is dependent upon acceptance of some reason for management to prefer valueless accounting. That preference seems indisputable, even if the reason(s) is in doubt. Another preference that seems indisputable is that of auditors' for good relations with the managements of client firms. It seems reasonable to speculate that many observers who are neither auditors nor managers of audited enterprises see auditors as lacking in independence of management, but willing to bend as far as they can to help managers "tell their story." *It follows that if managers prefer valueless accounting auditors prefer it.*

Auditors' Liability.-- The rationale here is that adherence to "transaction-based" values is safer because (1) it reduces the probability of a technical auditing failure related to lack of verifiability, fraud, and the like, (2) in the majority of cases valueless accounting gives lower, more conservative asset values, and auditors do not become liable for understatements, and (3) there would be some risks in changing over to value accounting. *Fear of liability could sway those auditors who see no particular merit in reporting wealth to owners and creditors.*

The Consistency Clause in the Auditor's Report.-- For several decades, the standard short-form audit report in the United States included a clause explicitly stating that the financial statements were prepared in accordance with generally accepted accounting principles applied on a basis consistent with that of the preceding year. Auditing standards required that, if that were not the case, an exception must be noted in the report. To the extent that such an exception was viewed as a flaw in the financial report, managements took pains to avoid it. Thus, there was a bias against change, so any mild preference for value accounting was resisted once valueless accounting was in place. Auditing standards continue to require disclosure of any change, even though the consistency clause no longer appears in the standard short-form report, so the bias against change continues. Auditing standards in Commonwealth countries include a similar requirement. *The consistency requirement has supported valueless accounting.*

Regulatory Explanations

Securities regulation and accounting regulation could play roles in the perpetuation of valueless accounting.

Securities Regulation.-- This explanation may be combined with others. Securities regulation at the national level began in the United States during the great depression when investors' losses were large and numerous, so fear of overstatement was genuine and pervasive. Consequently, one of the major thrusts of regulation was the prevention of overstatement of financial position and results. If that was the original accounting mission of the SEC, one can understand the bureaucracy's (and its clients') adherence to that pattern of thought even as the environment changes. In addition, the SEC's enforcement of accounting standards and the consistency clause in the auditor's report may well have strengthened the general resistance to change. *Securities regulation has supported valueless accounting.*

Accounting Regulation.-- Like securities regulation -- indeed, to some extent tied to it -- accounting regulation commenced in the U.S. during the great depression. Carmen Blough, the first chief accountant at the Securities and Exchange Commission, took office in December 1935. The American Institute of Accountants' Committee on Accounting Procedure was organized in 1938, and its first *Accounting Research Bulletin* was published in 1939. That first ARB included the Committee's acceptance of the six rules formally adopted by the Institute membership in 1934. The first of those rules was: "Unrealized profit should not be credited to income account of the corporations either directly or indirectly," thus outlawing upward revaluations of assets held.

One could suggest that accounting regulation was a factor that worked jointly with securities regulation, the consistency clause, and investors' conservatism to fix the practices of lower-of-cost-and-market valuation of current assets and historical cost valuation of fixed assets. With regulation came increasing influence of large companies and their auditors, so the innovative tendencies of smaller companies were suppressed. *The accounting regulatory process has delayed the adoption of value accounting.*

A Specific Failure of Standard Setters.-- Generally accepted accounting principles in the United States do not require the distinction between operating margins and gains and losses due to changing prices. Realized holding gains and losses on inventories and depreciable assets customarily are buried in the operating section of the income statement by reducing cost of goods sold and depreciation below their current cost levels. Gains and losses on sales of investments and plant assets generally do not qualify as extraordinary items or discontinuances of operations, and there is no clear-cut practice regarding their display as separate line items or their inclusion in a broad line item such as cost of goods sold or selling, general, and administrative expenses. Separate and clear disclosure of such items would reduce their value as instant earnings and losses. A consequence of poor reporting of price change gains and losses is that users of financial statements are not accustomed to making that distinction, so managers fear that separately-reported price-change gains and losses would be treated like operating margins as investors applied their price-earnings calculus to the company's financial results. Volatility is assumed to follow. Some observers believe that if accounting regulators had, early in the regulatory era, developed standards for distinguishing between, and reporting separately, operating margins and price changes, everyone concerned would now be more comfortable with reports of the price changes that inevitably accompany ownership of various kinds of assets in an uncertain world. So, *one explanation for adherence to valueless accounting is standards setters' failure to develop full disclosures of price change effects.*

Inertia

Old measurements came first. They are first in the bookkeeping sequence, and they apparently have been the general pattern over the history of double-entry bookkeeping. One might note that price changes have been much more pronounced in recent decades than they were in earlier centuries, so the practical difference between old and current measurements was not so great "in the old days." Therefore, *valueless accounting has custom, tradition, inertia on its side.* Change typically is resisted. According to John C. Burton's "Law of Anticipatory Multiplication:" "Every change is seen as several times more threatening in prospect than in retrospect." For example, it is much easier for teachers to continue to teach traditional methods than to tool up for a major change.

Omitted Explanations

Many hypotheses have been presented as possible explanations for the prevalence of valueless accounting. One may note that some of them appear to represent arguments rather than explanations -- points one might use in a debate in the hope that the judges will accept them. To any given reader, many of the explanations are bound to appear to be only debating points and will be rejected. Others may appear to be overstated or to have an argumentative element in them. But the intent in this chapter has been to include only explanations that were either defensible in the eyes of an objective observer (?) or were thought to be conscientiously believed by at least a few persons interested in the issue. The weight that each point may carry with a "judge" is a different matter which has not been addressed here.

Three popular arguments against value accounting that are excluded from the above listing of possible explanations for valueless accounting should be mentioned, along with the specific reasons for their exclusion. These three arguments are viewed as indirect arguments in the sense that they are used by people who have other reasons for opposing value accounting.

A frequently heard argument is that value accounting assumes liquidation of the enterprise rather than continuity. For example, in opposition to "mark-to-market accounting" for financial instruments: "This market value approach implies a 'fire sale' situation that is contrary to the 'going-concern' intention of management." (FEI, 1988, p. 2) That concern is not treated as an explanation for valueless accounting in this paper because switching from an entry value to an exit value was excluded from the paper's scope. The updating of values that is under discussion here includes use of current cost measurements or current market value of securities and certain graded commodities. Those measurements are not based on any assumption regarding a participant's reason for buying or selling. The argument that reporting current values assumes liquidation does not fit in this context.

Another argument that is omitted here is that updating the measurements of certain asset and liability items under circumstances that do not reasonably permit the updating of other net asset items introduces a lack of comparability. That assertion appears to be untrue because traditional valueless accounting provides for no comparability of measurement dates within a balance sheet. Monetary items are reported at approximately current values. Only by coincidence are two nonmonetary items measured as of the same date. The type of value accounting considered here would not involve any change in the fundamental nature of the valuations reported; they would represent observations of prices in the same markets relied upon in valueless accounting, with only the date of the price changed. The result would be greater comparability, because many -- at the limit, all -- net asset items would be measured at the same date -- the balance sheet date.

Finally, in the argument regarding marking debt securities owned to market, an intent on the part of management to hold those securities to maturity has been put forward as a reasons for reporting them at amortized cost. No reason is given why out-of-date values are preferable under that circumstance. Instead, distaste for income volatility usually is expressed. That explanation has been covered elsewhere in this chapter.

WHAT'S NEXT?

The preceding list of possible explanations for the prevalence of valueless accounting cannot be considered the end of the story, but all subsequent chapters are left to readers. Perhaps the most pertinent exercise at this point would be an attempt to relate the explanations offered above to the influences shaping the development of accounting in firms that have been emphasized in the earlier chapters. One leading question is offered: Which of the explanations suggested in this chapter cannot be associated with either (1) conflicts of interests, (2) costs of information, or (3) exogenous factors such as regulation or income taxation? In another "chapter," the reader may wish to attempt to organize the list of explanations by connecting them with interest groups. That exercise might lead one to speculate regarding who might prefer valueless accounting and for what reasons -- a modest step beyond the present work. To proceed to the point of identifying one primary interest group and its primary reason for preferring valueless accounting would be a big step -- one that surely would be quite subjective, as would speculations regarding which explanations sway standards setters. Sooner or later, anyone who is deeply committed to explaining why valueless accounting prevails must address the other question stated in the first section of this chapter. Who has the power to choose accounting methods?

One can, of course, feel free to make the academic's motherhood suggestion: further research in this area is encouraged. Testing the hypotheses presented here can challenge the most ambitious researchers. Another suggestion: responses to FASB discussion memoranda, exposure drafts and testimony at public hearings, along with similar presentations to the SEC, is a promising set of materials for study.

NOTES

1. Acceptance of a relatively strong form of the efficient market hypothesis could reduce the significance of the issue discussed here. If "the market" knew the make-up of the firm's "portfolio" of assets and liabilities and the prices of each item in that portfolio, financial reports showing current values of assets and liabilities would contribute little to the "market information set." To those who believe the market is efficient in that sense and who see no significant role for financial statement information beyond its contribution to the pricing of publicly traded securities, valueless accounting, like most accounting measurement alternatives, is not an issue.

2. An attempt to address a related issue -- mismatching -- is noteworthy. "When confronted with the blunt question of why a particular accounting practice continues to be followed, in spite of the confusion and misrepresentation of accounting data which it creates, the frank executive confesses that his accounting techniques are governed by one or more of the following: (1) tradition or established custom, which discourages change in accounting methods or financial statements in order to avoid confusion to employees or recipients of the company's statements; (2) conservatism; (3) cost involved in a change in methods; (4) tax savings; (5) lack of understanding of accounting principles; and (6) desire of management to present a particular financial picture." (Blocker, 1949, p. 33)

CHAPTER 8
CONCLUDING NOTES

On these few pages a few points are emphasized that have been treated too lightly or completely overlooked in the body of the work. One exercise that ought to be considered is reverse tracing of the relationships between economic features of firms and the major concepts that are recognized in accounting. Accounting principles, assumptions, doctrines, conventions, and practices become the starting point in this exercise; the most important influences shaping their development are to be matched with those concepts.

Another matter to be considered here is the general area of omitted influences. Several historical developments and current features of the firm environment that the reader might consider relevant are addressed in the second section. A comment on the symbiotic relationship between accounting and the economics of the firm follows, and the chapter concludes with speculations on the unevenness of progress in accounting in the past and present.

The Association of Accounting Concepts with Features of Firms

The tabular listing on the next page shows an informal list of concepts that frequently are emphasized in accounting literature. No attempt is made here to classify those concepts as principles, assumptions, doctrines, conventions, practices or some other class of important ideas. The objective is to show

CONVENTIONAL ACCOUNTING CONCEPTS AND FIRM FEATURES INFLUENCING THEIR DEVELOPMENT

Accounting Concept	Influences on Development of Concept
Accounting equation	Definition of firm
Accruals, deferrals	Definition, externalities
Comparability	Performance evaluation
Conservatism	Conflicts of interests
Consistency	Conflicts of interests
Continuity	Definition of firm
Cost valuation	Conflicts, asset uniqueness
Double entry	Definition, opportunism, etc.
Entity	Definition of firm
Estimation	Definition, indivisibilities
Full disclosure	Conflicts of interests
Internal check	Opportunism, size, etc.
Materiality	Information cost, bounded rationality
Neutrality	Conflicts, opportunism
Nominal dollars	Conflicts of interests
Performance reporting	Performance evaluation, size
Periodic reporting	Conflicts of interests
Product costing	Diversification, integration, etc.
Proprietary view	Definition of firm
Realization	Conflicts of interests
Return on investment	Form of organization
Verifiability	Opportunism, conflicts

that every important concept on a reasonably inclusive list can be traced to one or more of the "influences" -- features of firms and their activities -- shown in EXHIBIT 1 on page 149. Not every concept-influence connection that appears in the text is listed here, due to space limitations, but the most important ones are. For example, additional influences easily could be identified in the cases of such pervasive concepts as the accounting equation, accruals and deferrals, double entry, estimation, internal check, performance reporting, and product costing. Also, one might observe that all refinements of cash basis accounting -- accruals, deferrals, estimations, product costing -- can be attributed to firm constituents' demands for better measurements of wealth and income.

The abbreviated statements of the accounting concepts could be troublesome in a few cases. Accruals and deferrals are intended to encompass the matching concept. Nominal dollars means that the measuring unit is assumed to be stable; no price level adjustments are needed. Continuity often has been referred to as the going concern assumption. Cost valuation is an abbreviation for the general use of acquisition cost in the measurement of nonmonetary assets. Estimation covers such matters as uncollectible receivables, product warranty liabilities, pension costs, and depreciation and amortization. Performance reporting includes such practices as comparisons of actual results against budgets and standards as well as responsibility accounting. Product costing includes the distinction between direct and indirect costs, predetermined overhead rates, allocations, and so on. Less conventional concepts, such as market simulation accounting, are omitted here.

Omitted Influences

One category of important influences shaping the development of accounting was omitted because they are exogenous in the context of a study of the economics of the firm. Income taxation and regulation of accounting and auditing are imposed on the firm from outside rather than evolving naturally from within. For those who find their exclusion unsettling, several hypotheses regarding their influence are offered:

1. Starting with the emphasis on codification of accounting standards and regulation of financial reporting in the United States in the 1930s, methods used for determining income for external reporting have dominated those used for internal reporting.

2. Because today's accounting practices have been chosen almost entirely by managements, one can expect the status quo to prevail to a substantial extent as long as management dominates the "standards-setting process."

3. Voluntary changes in firms' external reporting practices -- especially changes in a conservative direction without a tax advantage -- have been rare since the consistency clause was added to the standard auditor's opinion.

4. The rise of legal and regulatory requirements in accounting has diverted the attention and efforts of talented accountants from serving noncompelling internal uses to meeting, avoiding, and resisting requirements, thereby stifling innovations in management accounting. (Johnson and Kaplan, 1987, p. 260)

5. Income taxation has had significant influences on firms' operating activities and on the extent of record keeping, especially in small firms, but has stimulated relatively few changes in the measurement of enterprise wealth and income in large firms. It may serve as a drag on the evolution of information systems for management.

A broader approach to omitted influences would start with ancient history and would extend far afield. Again, some readers are likely to be deeply interested in such an approach.

ACCOUNTING IN THE HISTORY OF THE WORLD

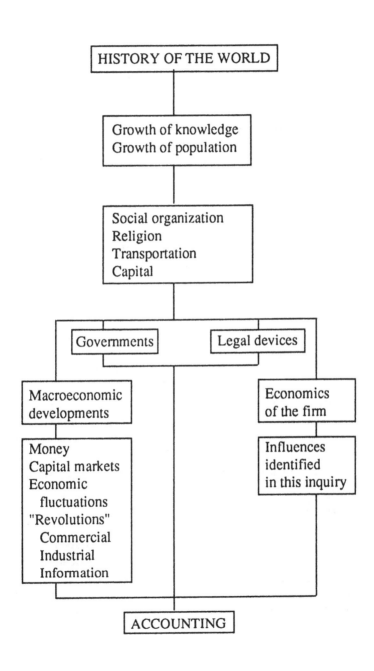

The current version of a constantly evolving outline of that type is presented on page 145. Readers versed in accounting history will note a debt to Littleton (1929, Ch. II).

Incomplete markets and imperfect markets are other economic phenomena that have been largely ignored in this study. Their importance to accounting cannot be denied. With complete and perfect markets, interested parties would be able to observe a price for every asset and liability of a firm, including intangibles and contingencies, and those prices would be as acceptable as the "best" of our up-to-the-minute quotations for widely-traded commodities and securities. (Think of the confidence that mutual fund investors place in securities quotations when they buy and sell fund shares at their net asset values.) One might be tempted to say that all of the problems of accounting would be absent in a regime of complete and perfect markets. But those features of our economies are not endogenous features of firms, so they are not parts of this study.

Finally, some readers are bound to be puzzled by the omission of uncertainty as an influence on the development of accounting. It clearly is pervasive in its influence; without uncertainty, what accounting would be wanted? "In a world of uncertainty, information becomes a useful commodity." (Hirshleifer, 1970, p. 311) But uncertainty does not appear to be peculiarly related to the economics of the firm. If one were to attempt to identify its influence on firm accounting, what could be said? Does firm accounting owe its existence to uncertainty?

Symbiotic Relationships

The four influences shown in tier 3 of EXHIBIT I, page 149, -- size of firm, vertical integration, diversification, and form of organization -- are sometimes referred to as size, strategy and structure. The relationships among them and between them and accounting have not been investigated as thoroughly as one might like in this inquiry. The focus has been on their influences on the development of accounting in firms. A slightly broader view is that as firms made modest advances in size, expansion strategy, or structure, accounting responded to meet the expanded needs for information. Then, accounting's responses permitted further advances in size, strategy, and/or structure. Thus, simple growth in firm size and movements towards vertical integration, diversification and multi-divisional organizations occurred partly as a consequence of accounting development. These symbiotic relationships might be limited to the tier 3 influences, although one could also argue that performance evaluation and use of incentive plans both influenced accounting and were influenced by accounting's response. Symbiotic relationships deserve more attention.

One More Hypothesis

Advances in accounting appear to have occurred unevenly over time. The same observation might be made regarding other fields and the growth of knowledge in general. In the case of accounting, the period when double-entry bookkeeping was developed -- presumably the fourteenth century -- might be considered a period of major advancement. Another general period with substantial advances encompassed roughly the period between 1880 and 1940. Advances in managerial accounting devices, development of consolidated financial statements, more use of estimates, and exposition of theoretical issues in the literature marked this period. Since 1940, it is difficult to find new developments except for applications to newly important financial features (pensions, income taxation, foreign currency) of accounting techniques that were developed earlier. Several hypotheses could be advanced for the twentieth century stagnant period in accounting; take your choice:

1.   Two major regulatory influences received priority: income taxation and the setting of financial reporting

standards. The pressure of compliance with those firm requirements swamped any low-priority interest in information for traditional purposes.

2.   During the earlier periods of substantial advances in accounting the routine work of accounting did not challenge the intellectual capacities and interests of the well-qualified "men" involved in it, so they sought intellectual satisfaction in developing new ideas related to their work. Since 1940, however, the complex challenges posed by income tax regulations, new accounting standards from regulators, technological advances in data processing, and additional government regulations and legal requirements in closely related matters to which practicing accountants often are assigned, have left accountants exhausted and yearning for simpler and familiar solutions rather than seeking novelty. This can be called "the full plate hypothesis."

3.   The lack of evolution in techniques for measuring entity wealth and income may be due to the switch in importance in the economy from owner-controlled firms to management-controlled firms, thus emphasizing the conflict between the interests of managers and the interests of owners, especially the types of biases discussed in Chapter 4.

Conclusion

History has not reached its terminus. None of the influences on the development of accounting in firms that have been identified in this book have completed their work. This is a story of historical development in progress. Perhaps certain of the influences discussed here have little to offer in the future. Others may be in the midst of their impacts, and still others just beginning theirs. Are there unrecognized potential influences that have not yet started to play their roles? The safest conclusion seems to be: this is a story without end.

EXHIBIT I

MAJOR ECONOMIC FEATURES OF FIRMS INFLUENCING THE DEVELOPMENT OF ACCOUNTING

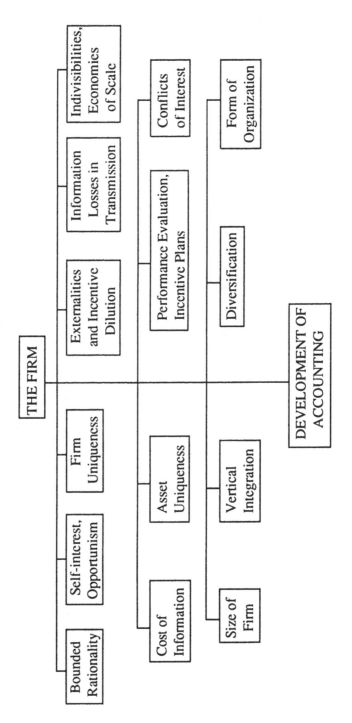

REFERENCES

Akerlof, G., "The Market for 'Lemons': Quality, Uncertainty and the Market Mechanism," *Quarterly Journal of Economics*, August 1970, pp. 488-500.

Alchian, A. A., "Private Property and the Relative Cost of Tenure," in Philip D. Bradley, ed., *The Public Stake in Union Power* (Charlottesville, VA: The University Press of Virginia, 1958), pp. 350-371.

_____, "First National Maintenance vs. National Labor Relations Board," unpublished manuscript, 1982.

_____, and H. Demsetz, "Production, Information Costs, and Economic Organization," *American Economic Review*, December, 1972, pp. 777-795.

_____, and S. Woodward, "Reflections on the Theory of the Firm," *Journal of Institutional and Theoretical Economics*, 1987, No. 1, pp. 110-37.

_____, "The Firm is Dead: Long Live the Firm: Review of Oliver E. Williamson's The Economic Institutions of Capitalism," *Journal of Economic Literature*, March 1988, pp. 65-79.

American Institute of Accountants, Committee on Accounting Procedure, 1939. *Accounting Research Bulletin* No. 1, "General Introduction and Rules Formerly Adopted," September.

Archibald, G.C., "Theory of the Firm," in J.M. Eatwell, M. Milgate and P. Newman (eds.), *The New Palgrave: A Dictionary of Economics* (New York: The Stockton Press, 1987), Vol. II, pp. 357-363.

Argyris, C., "Human Problems with Budgets," *Harvard Business Review*, January-February 1953.

Armstrong, M. S., "The Politics of Establishing Accounting Standards," *Journal of Accountancy*, February 1977, pp. 76-79.

Arrow, K., Lecture at the University of California at Berkeley, April 7, 1988.

Baiman, S., "Agency Research in Managerial Accounting; A Second Look," Unpublished, Carnegie-Mellon University, 1989.

Ball, R. J., "The Firm as a Specialist Contracting Intermediary: Application to Accounting and Auditing," Unpublished, University of Rochester, 1989.

_____ and C. Smith, *The Economics of Accounting Policy Choice* (New York: Mc-Graw Hill, 1992).

Bartlett, F.C., *Remembering* (Cambridge, England: The Cambridge University Press, 1932).

Barzel, Y., "Measurement Costs and the Organization of Markets," *Journal of Law and Economics*, April 1982, pp. 27-48.

Berle, A. A., and G. C. Means, *The Modern Corporation and Private Property* (New York: The Macmillan Company, 1932).

Blair, R.D., and D.L. Kaserman, *Law and Economics of Vertical Integration and Control* (New York and London: Academic Press, 1983).

Blocker, J. G., "Mismatching of Costs and Revenues," *The Accounting Review*, January 1949, pp. 33-43.

Boulding, K.E., "The Economics of Knowledge and the Knowledge of Economics," *American Economic Review*, May 1968, pp. 1-13.

Buchanan, J.M., "Rent Seeking and Profit Seeking," in J.M. Buchanan, D. Tollison, G. Tullock (eds.), *Towards a Theory of the Rent-Seeking Society* (College Station, TX: Texas A&M University, 1980).

Buchanan, N.S., *The Economics of Corporate Enterprise* (New York: Henry Holt and Co., 1940).

Butterworth, J. E., M. Gibbins, and R. D. King, "The Structure of Accounting Theory: Some Basic Conceptual and Methodological Issues," *Research to Support Standard Setting in Financial Accounting: A Canadian Perspective* (Toronto: Clarkson Gordon Foundation, 1982), pp. 1-65.

Chandler, A.D., Jr., *Strategy and Structure* (Garden City, NY: Doubleday and Co., 1962).

_____, *The Visible Hand* (Cambridge, MA: The Belknap Press of the Harvard University Press, 1977).

Cheung, S.N.S., "The Contractual Nature of the Firm," *Journal of Law and Economics*, April 1983, pp. 1-21.

Coase, R.H., "The Nature of the Firm," *Economica*, 1937, pp. 386-405.

_____, "Business Organization and the Accountant," *The Accountant*, October 1 - December 17, 1938.

_____, "Accounting and the Theory of the Firm," *Journal of Accounting and Economics*, January 1990, pp. 1-11.

_____, R. Edwards and R.F. Fowler, "Published Balance Sheets as an Aid to Economic Investigation -- Some Difficulties," *Publications of the Accounting Research Association* (London: Gee & Co., Ltd., June 1938).

Cobb, C.W., and P.H. Douglas, "A Theory of Production," *American Economic Review*, March 1928, pp. 139-165.

DeSerpa, A.C., *Microeconomic Theory: Issues and Applications* (Boston: Allyn and Bacon, Inc., 1985).

Downs, A., *Inside Bureaucracy* (Boston: Little, Brown, 1967).

Drucker, P., "The Futures That Have Already Happened," *The Economist*, October 21, 1989, pp. 19-22.

Edwards, R.S., "The Rationale of Cost Accounting," in A. Plant (ed.), *Some Modern Business Problems* (London: Longmans Green & Co., Ltd., 1937), pp. 275-299.

Financial Accounting Standards Board, *Statements of Financial Accounting Concepts*, No. 2, "Qualitative Characteristics of Accounting Information," FASB, 1980.

_____, *Statements of Financial Accounting Standards*, Series, 1973-.

Financial Executive Institute, *FEI Briefing*, June 1988, p. 2.

Florence, P.S., *The Logic of Industrial Organisation* (London: Kegan Paul, Trench, Frubner & Co., 1933).

Geneen, H., "The Case for Managing by the Numbers," *Fortune*, October 1, 1984, pp. 78-81.

Georgescu-Roegen, N., *The Entropy Law and Economic Process* (Cambridge, MA: Harvard University Press, 1971).

Govindarajan, V., and R. Anthony, "How Firms Use Cost Data in Price Decisions," *Management Accounting*, July 1983, pp. 30-36.

Grossman, S.J., and O.D. Hart, "The Costs and Benefits of Ownership: A Theory of Vertical and Lateral Integration," *Journal of Political Economy*, August 1986, pp. 691-719.

Hamilton, R., *An Introduction to Merchandize*, printed for the author, Edinburgh, 1777-1779.

Harris, J.N., "What Did We Earn Last Month?" *NACA Bulletin*, January 15, 1936, pp. 501-527.

Healy, P. M., "The Effects of Bonus Schemes on Accounting Decisions," *Journal of Accounting and Economics*, 1985, pp. 85-107.

Hirshleifer, J., *Investment, Interest and Capital* (Englewood Cliffs, NJ: Prentice-Hall, 1970).

Holmstrum, B., "Agency Costs and Innovation," Working Paper, Yale University, August 1988.

Jaques, E., *Time-Span Handbook* (London: Heinemann, 1966).

Jensen, M., and W. Meckling, "Theory of the Firm: Managerial Behavior, Agency Costs, and Capital Structure," *Journal of Financial Economics*, October 1976, pp. 305-360.

Johnson, H.T., "The Search for Gain in Markets and Firms: A Review of the Historical Emergence of Management

Accounting Systems," *Accounting, Organizations and Society*, 1983, pp. 139-146.

_____ and R.S. Kaplan, *Relevance Lost: The Rise and Fall of Management Accounting* (Boston: Harvard Business School Press, 1987).

Kaldor, N., "The Equilibrium of the Firm," *Economic Journal*, March 1934, pp. 60-76.

Kaplan, R.S., "Strategic Cost Analysis," in *Cost Accounting for the 90s* (Montvale, NJ: National Association of Accountants, 1986), pp. 129-140.

Kelly-Newton, L., *Accounting Policy Formulation: The Role of Corporate Management* (Reading, MA: Addison-Wesley, 1980).

Laffont, J.J., "Externalities," in J.M. Eatwell, M. Milgate and P. Newman (eds.), *The New Palgrave: A Dictionary of Economics* (New York: The Stockton Press, 1987), Vol. 2, pp. 263-265.

Leonard, J., "Executive Pay and Firm Performance," *Industrial and Labor Relations Review*, February 1990, pp. 13-29.

Littleton, A.C., *Accounting Evolution to 1900* (New York: American Institute Publishing Co., Inc., 1933).

Lynch, P., *One Up on Wall Street* (New York: Penguin Books, 1989).

Marschak, J., "Money and the Theory of Assets," *Econometrica*, October 1938, pp. 311-325.

_____, and R. Radner, *Economic Theory of Teams* (New Haven, CT: Yale University Press, 1972).

Marshall, A., *Principles of Economics*, 3rd Ed. (London: Macmillan and Co., 1895).

_____, *Principles of Economics*, 8th edition (London: MacMillan and Co., 1920).

Masten, S.E., "The Economic Institutions of Capitalism: A Review Article," *Journal of Institutional and Theoretical Economics*, June 1986, pp. 445-451.

Masten, S.E., J.W. Meehan and E.A. Snyder, "The Costs of Organization," *Journal of Law, Economics and Organization*, April 1991, pp. 1-25.

McCullers, L.D., and W.R. McDill, "'Quasi-Pricing' for Intracompany Transactions," *The Journal of Accountancy*, December 1970, pp. 80-82.

Mepham, M.J., "The Eighteenth-Century Origins of Cost Accounting," *Abacus*, March 1988, pp. 55-70.

Mill, J., *Elements of Political Economy* (London: Baldwin, Cradock, and Joy, 1821).

Mill, J. S., *Principles of Political Economy* (1849), Vol. II, *Collected Works of John Stuart Mill* (Toronto: University of Toronto Press, 1965).

Niskanen, W.A., *Bureaucracy and Representative Government* (Chicago: Aldine-Antherton, 1971).

Olson, M.L., "Towards a More General Theory of Governmental Structure," *American Economic Review*, May 1986, pp. 120-125.

Papandreou, A.G., "Some Problems in the Theory of the Firm," in F. Haley (ed.), *A Survey of Contemporary Economics*, II (Homewood, IL: Richard D. Irwin, Inc., 1952).

Penrose, E.T., *The Theory of the Growth of the Firm* (New York: John Wiley & Sons, Inc., 1959).

Pigou, A.C., *Economics of Welfare* (London: MacMillan & Co., 1920).

Ricardo, D., *Principles of Political Economy and Taxation*, 3rd edition (London: George Bell and Sons, 1821).

Robinson, E.A.G., *The Structure of Competitive Industry* (London: Nisbet & Co., 1931).

deRoover, R., "The Development of Accounting Prior to Luca Pacioli According to the Account-Books of Medieval Merchants," in A.C. Littleton and B. Yamey, *Studies in the History of Accounting* (London: Sweet & Maxwell, Ltd., 1956), pp. 114-175.

Rumelt, R.P., *Strategy, Structure, and Economic Performance* (Boston: Harvard Business School Press, 1986). (Originally published by Richard D. Irwin, 1974.)

Schipper, K., "Earnings Management," *Accounting Horizons*, December 1989, pp. 91-102.

Simon, H.E., *Models of Man* (New York: John Wiley & Sons, 1957).

Smith, A., *An Inquiry into the Nature and Causes of the Wealth of Nations* (1776), reprinted in two volumes, Campbell, Skinner, and Todd (eds.), (Oxford: Clarendon Press, 1976).

Smith, C. and J. Warner, "On Financial Contracting: An Analysis of Bond Covenants," *Journal of Financial Economics*, June 1979, pp. 117-161.

Sombart, W., "Medieval and Modern Commercial Enterprise," in F.C. Lane and J. Riemersma, *Enterprise and Secular Change* (Homewood, IL: Richard D. Irwin, 1953). Trans. of *Der Moderne Kapitalismus*, 6th ed. (Munich & Leipzig: Von Duncker & Humblot, 1924).

Stamp, Sir J., "Industrial Profits in the Past Twenty Years: A New Index Number," *Journal of the Royal Statistical Society*, 1932, p. 660.

Staubus, G.J., *A Theory of Accounting to Investors* (Berkeley: University of California Press, 1961).

_____, *Activity Costing and Input-Output Accounting* (Homewood, IL: Richard D. Irwin, Inc., 1971).

_____, "An Induced Theory of Accounting Measurement," *The Accounting Review*, January 1985, pp. 53-75.

_____, "The Market Simulation Theory of Accounting Measurement," *Accounting and Business Research*, Spring 1986, pp. 117-132.

_____, *Activity Costing for Decisions* (New York: Garland Publishing, Inc., 1988).

_____, 1989.

Stigler, G.J., *The Theory of Price* (New York: MacMillan & Co., 1947).

Stinson, C. H., "Net Worth Requirements and Management of Provisions for Losses in Savings and Loans," Unpublished Paper, Stanford University, 1991.

Teece, D.J., "Economies of Scope and the Scope of the Enterprise," *Journal of Economic Behavior and Organization*, 1980, pp. 223-238.

_____, "Technological Change and the Nature of the Firm," Working Paper no. EAP-22, Center for Research in Management, University of California at Berkeley, 1987.

_____, Lecture, University of California at Berkeley, February 25, 1988.

Thompson, A.A., *Economics of the Firm: Theory and Practice*, 3rd edition (Englewood Cliffs, NJ: Prentice-Hall, Inc., 1981).

Thompson, J.D., *Organizations in Action* (New York: McGraw-Hill, 1967).

Tullock, G., *The Politics of Bureaucracy* (Washington: Public Affairs Press, 1965).

Vancil, R.F., *Decentralization: Managerial Ambiguity by Design* (Homewood, IL: Dow Jones-Irwin, 1978).

Wall Street Journal, "Labor Letter," February 21, 1989, p. A-1.

_____, "Managing Profits: How General Electric Damps Fluctuations in Its Annual Earnings," November 3, 1994, pp. A1, A8.

Watts, R.L., and J.L. Zimmerman, *Positive Accounting Theory* (Englewood Cliffs, NJ: Prentice-Hall, Inc., 1986).

Williamson, O.F., *Corporate Control and Business Behavior* (Englewood Cliffs, NJ: Prentice-Hall, Inc., 1970).

_____, "The Vertical Integration of Production: Market Failure Considerations," *American Economic Review*, May 1971, pp. 112-127.

_____, *The Economic Institutions of Capitalism: Firms, Markets, Relational Contracting* (New York: The Free Press, 1985).

_____, "Corporate Finance and Corporate Governance," unpublished working paper, Center for Research in Management, University of California, Berkeley, 1987.

_____, "The Logic of Economic Organization," *Journal of Law, Economics, and Organization*, Spring 1988, pp. 65-93.

_____, "Operationalizing the New Institutional Economics," Unpublished Working Paper, University of California at Berkeley, 1989.

INDEX